LIVERPOOL JOHN LENNON AIRPORT
AN ILLUSTRATED HISTORY

LIVERPOOL JOHN LENNON AIRPORT
AN ILLUSTRATED HISTORY

PHIL BUTLER

TEMPUS

Frontispiece: The new control tower at Liverpool Airport, officially opened in 2002. This is another development made by Liverpool Airport PLC following the takeover by Peel Holdings. As with the terminal developments, the construction was partly financed by European Union Objective One funding. (Adrian Thompson)

First published 2004
This edition 2008

Tempus Publishing
Cirencester Road, Chalford,
Stroud, Gloucestershire, GL6 8PE
www.tempus-publishing.com

Tempus Publishing is an imprint of The History Press Ltd

British Library Cataloguing in Publication Data.
A catalogue record for this book is available from the British Library.

ISBN 978 0 7524 4511 3

Typesetting and origination by The History Press Ltd
Printed in Great Britain

Contents

Foreword

I do not think that Blériot could possibly have imagined what he was starting when he crossed the English Channel from France to England in July 1909. Aviation has now become one of the fastest growing and most successful industries worldwide and is forecast to continue expanding for the foreseeable future. Liverpool Airport has had a chequered history, leading the way in the early years of municipal airports, and becoming a thriving aerodrome at Speke following its opening in 1933. It also played a very important part during the war years, but then lack of foresight and investment subsequently handed the initiative to Manchester Airport.

More recent years have seen an acceleration in the development of regional airports, brought about by an increasing demand to fly. The mass market and technical developments by the major aircraft manufacturers have provided increasing numbers of aircraft and the opportunity for airports with a significant catchment area, such as Liverpool, to develop. The privatisation of airports, following the passing of the Airports Act 1986, resulted in the sale of Liverpool Airport to British Aerospace (1990) and subsequently to Peel Holdings (1997), which has provided much needed direction and investment. Certainly, a more commercial approach, with the rebranding of the airport as Liverpool John Lennon Airport in 2002 has played its part in re-establishing a significant role for the airport in the north west.

Another important factor has been the evolution of the low-cost carriers, which has challenged the established role of the traditional carriers in the market place. Demand for a well-positioned airport in the north west offering highly competitive charging and handling arrangements has given a major boost to Liverpool's air traffic. More importantly, with increased numbers of flights and destinations available to the public, critical mass and economies of scale have been achieved which should provide Liverpool John Lennon Airport with a secure future. It will certainly make an increasingly important contribution to the Merseyside economy in the years to come.

This book provides a fascinating insight into the development of a regional airport which has faced many challenges and is now well placed to meet the future with confidence.

Rod Hill, formerly Managing Director, Liverpool Airport PLC, 1992–2002

Preface and Acknowledgements

Since the publication of the previous edition of this book, there have been many new developments, so now is the time to bring the history up to date. Although most of the new material covers the intervening period, from 2003 to 2007, some new material has been unearthed about earlier days, in particular about the First World War aerodrome at Aintree, which was used for aircraft manufacture from 1917 to 1919 and then received some pioneering airline flights during the 1920s. More material has also been found on the Rootes aircraft factory of the Second World War. However, the main new material concerns the quite dramatic expansion of passenger traffic at Liverpool John Lennon Airport, which has been driven by the 'low-cost' carriers easyJet, Ryanair and Wizz Air over the last few years.

Much of the material from the previous edition has been retained, with some minor corrections, while some of the additional photographs included in this book refer to the earlier periods in the airport's history as well as the latest developments. Feedback from the last edition revealed that some readers were disappointed that no mention had been made of the several air displays which had taken place over the years, and I have tried to respond to this by the inclusion of an account of the 1956 Whit Monday display, prepared by fellow enthusiast Don Stephens. Also included is a list of other Liverpool air displays, prepared by Brian Jones, and I am most grateful for the help of both Don and Brian for these and their other contributions, and to Ken Roberts for the original suggestion and material.

As before, the overall work was carried out or co-ordinated by Phil Butler, the author of the earlier history, but many others made useful contributions, including the late Barry Abraham, Keith Crowden, Dave Graham, Mike Lewis and Adrian Thompson. Thanks are due to Ossie Jones for preparation of the plan of the Aintree aircraft factory and airfield. Thanks are also extended to Robin Tudor (business services manager of Liverpool Airport PLC) and his assistant Clare Nelson for their help and support. Items credited to the Phil Butler collection comprise the former archive of the Merseyside Aviation Society, or more recent additions to it. Finally, I am also grateful to Dave Blackburn and Graham Ward for contributions about The Jetstream Club and the Friends of Liverpool Airport, respectively

Although we have tried to use new photographs wherever possible, the scarcity of items has sometimes left no alternative but to use those that appeared in the first edition. The Brian Andrews collection has therefore again been a prime source of material. Brian Jones, George Jones and Dave Smith (who were among those consulted during the production of the first edition) have had their archives and brainpower drawn on once more. Among the main sources, the Air-Britain Merseyside journal *North West Air News* has been scoured for many items of detail, as has the former MAS journal *EGGP* and the FoLA journal *09/27*. Via the good offices of the Friends of Liverpool Airport (FoLA), we have been able to draw on a photograph collection dating from 1933 (with thanks to Graham Ward and Alan Thelwell). Other photographic material has come from the collections of Norman Anyon, Phil Dale, Aldon Ferguson, Ken Fielding, Bill Hodgson, Ian Keast, Gerry Manning, Don Stephens and Adrian Thompson, as acknowledged in the captions, while I also thank Catherine Gow of the Littlewoods Organisation for additional photographs. The author welcomes any relevant additional photographs of buildings, aircraft and personalities for use in later editions.

As well as the Rootes Group archive held by the Museum of British Road Transport in Coventry, which earlier provided a real gold mine of new material and photographs on the Rootes-managed aircraft 'Shadow Factory' that operated on the edge of the airport from 1937–45, further gems have been provided with the help of Harry Fraser-Mitchell of the Handley Page Association. We extend our thanks to Harry and to the Road Transport Museum archivist, Barry Collins, for their much-appreciated assistance. The Rootes Group and Handley Page Association archives hold collections of photographs originally taken by a Liverpool company, Palatine Studios – anyone knowing of the location of Palatine's own archives is invited to get in touch with the author. Thanks are also due to Paul Francis for an excellent map of the airport as it was in 1945.

As before, we acknowledge reference to the long out-of-print *British Independent Airlines since 1946* (now reissued as *British Independent Airlines 1946–1976*, ISBN 0 907178 82 0), and the equally invaluable but more recent Air-Britain publications *Royal Air Force Flying Training and Support Units* (ISBN 0 85130 252 1) and *The Squadrons of the Fleet Air Arm* (ISBN 0 85130 223 8).

Introduction

The very first version of this history, published by the Merseyside Aviation Society, was prepared for the fiftieth anniversary of the official opening of the airport in July 1933. An entirely new book was produced by the present publisher in 2004, and this new significantly expanded edition brings the story up to date, charting the many changes that have taken place during the intervening period up to 2007, when major developments at the airport provided a fitting occasion once again to take stock of the history. Earlier developments, including the official renaming of Liverpool John Lennon Airport and the opening of the splendid new terminal building were covered in the 2004 book, but the expansion of traffic and the facilities to cope with this growth are now included to bring the picture up to date prior to the 75th anniversary of the official opening of the original Liverpool Airport on 1 July 1933.

The first recognisable airfield serving Liverpool was prepared during the First World War. During the war many firms became involved in aircraft construction; the new technology of aviation drew in manufacturers from a wide variety of backgrounds. So it was that in November 1917, the Cunard Steamship Company was given a contract to build 500 Bristol F.2B fighters at a factory at Aintree, adjacent to the racecourse. In total, 126 Bristol fighters were flown from a flying ground adjacent to the racecourse before production ceased in 1919. A fuller account of the Cunard factory (National Aircraft Factory No.3) appears in this edition of the book following recent research. In 1924 a concern called Northern Air Lines started a daily airmail service from Aintree to Belfast, using aircraft of the de Havilland Aeroplane Hire Service. Passengers could also be carried for a single fare of £3. The service ran from 30 April to 2 June, when it was abandoned because the state of the aerodromes at both ends of the route did not allow the company to run a reliable service.

In 1927 the Liverpool Organisation, a publicity and promotions organisation partly financed by Liverpool City Council, began to lobby for the development of a municipal aerodrome. Around this time the Air Ministry was actively promoting the development of such facilities by writing to local authorities suggesting that they were necessary. This arose partly from a general thrust of promoting 'air-mindedness' in members of the public, but was linked to the provision of additional facilities without cost to the Air Ministry which might be available for use in time of war or

The Short Calcutta flying-boat G-EBVH of Imperial Airways on the Mersey in September 1928, during the experimental Liverpool–Belfast air service sponsored by the Liverpool Organisation. (Phil Butler collection)

other emergencies. By April 1928, the Liverpool and District Aero Club had been formed (subsidised by the Air Ministry), but this operated from Hooton Park, another racecourse that had become an airfield during the First World War, because of the lack of aviation facilities within the boundary of the city.

On 1 August 1928, Liverpool City Council decided to purchase the Speke Estate of 2,200 acres from the executors of its former owner, Miss Adelaide Watt, for the development of housing and industrial estates for the city, but also with the possible provision of a municipal aerodrome in mind. In February 1929 government sanction for a loan of £162,150 to purchase 1,726 acres of land was received, the balance of the area being bought later, in 1933.

In September 1928, the Liverpool Organisation sponsored the operation of an experimental mail and passenger service from Liverpool to Belfast. This was operated by a Short Calcutta flying boat of Imperial Airways, flying from the River Mersey; after a demonstration flight on 22 September, the service operated from 24 September to 4 October. The Liverpool marine aerodrome was operated by the Mersey Docks and Harbour Board; although it continued as a licensed aerodrome for a number of years up to the Second World War, no other commercial operations have been traced. The marine aerodrome was bounded to the north by a line due east from Rock Ferry Pier, and to the south by a line running due west from a point in Garston Docks.

The Very First Liverpool Aerodrome at Aintree

As mentioned in the Introduction, the first recognised aerodrome in Liverpool was that prepared at Aintree in 1917 for 'National Aeroplane Factory No.3', which was to be managed on behalf of the First World War Ministry of Munitions by the Cunard Steamship Company. The site was chosen because several other 'national' factories already existed in the immediate area, the scheme having been set up at the behest of Prime Minister Lloyd George to respond to public criticism of inadequate supplies of munitions (at first, primarily artillery shells) reaching British troops in France. The Ministry of Munitions of War was set up to deal with the problem, and when a large network of factories had been built to make shells, cartridge cases and the explosives to fill them, attention was turned to building more aircraft as the Royal Flying Corps, and its successor the Royal Air Force, expanded beyond the capacity of existing factories to supply the necessary materiel. Apart from the other 'national' factories nearby, a prime reason for choosing the particular site was the nearby railway station (for access by the workforce) and the ability to build a railway spur to cater for incoming material.

The Cunard company became involved in discussions with the Aeroplane Construction Department of the Ministry of Munitions in February 1917, after the Ministry enquired whether the Furnishing Department of Cunard could assist with aeroplane manufacture. The Furnishing Department existed to fit out the passenger accommodation of steam ships ordered by the shipping line, installing the cabins and public areas of the ships into the hulls provided by Cammell Lairds, Harland & Wolff and other shipbuilders, and maintaining and re-fitting them when in service.

After lengthy negotiations, a definite scheme was formulated in July 1917 and Cunard agreed to manage the construction and operation of a factory, and work began on the design and building of the Aintree site on land purchased from the Earl of Sefton and adjacent to one of the existing National Munitions works. The Aintree works was NAF No.3, from an initial plan for four such factories (No.1 being at Croydon, No.2 was planned at Richmond in Surrey, and No.4 at Heaton Chapel, Stockport). In the end, the planned No.2 was dropped and the Stockport factory became No.2. The

This photograph shows one of the Aintree-built Bristol F.2B Fighters, numbered D2222. The shape of the long engine exhaust confirms that this one was fitted with a Sunbeam Arab engine. (G. Stuart Leslie collection, courtesy of the Fleet Air Arm Museum)

The management staff of the NAF at the time of the factory opening in 1918. The uniformed gentleman in the centre of the picture is believed to be Major Butler-Stoney, the factory manager. (Courtesy of University of Liverpool Library)

original name was 'National Aeroplane Factory', but the term 'Aeroplane' seems to have been used interchangeably with 'Aircraft' in contemporary correspondence.

Cunard received a copy of the preliminary plans for NAF No.1 early in September 1917 as a basis to start construction of its own factory, although the type of aircraft to be made at No.3 had still not been decided. Factory construction started on 4 October 1917 with 'cutting the first sod' on the site. The nucleus of the Aeroplane Department of Cunard was being set up in the Cunard Headquarters Building at Liverpool Pier Head, with staff seconded from the company's Engineering and Furnishing Departments. The company was informed that the aircraft to be built would be the the de Havilland D.H.9, but within a few days it became clear that the first order would be the Bristol F.2B, to become famous as the 'Bristol Fighter'.

The contract was for 500 Bristol F.2B Fighters, intended to be powered by Hispano-Suiza 8B engines of 200 h.p., rather than the Rolls-Royce Falcon or Sunbeam Arab engines usually fitted. Because of problems that delayed delivery of the intended engines, some aircraft were delivered without engines, and most others were fitted with the Sunbeam Arab. Eventually, only 126 of the intended F.2Bs were completed, following the November 1918 Armistice and the resulting cancellation of most existing contracts for aircraft. The first F.2B was completed on 7 June 1918 and production ceased in January 1919. The serial numbers of the aircraft were D2126 to D2625, with those after D2252 being cancelled. The contract specified that the

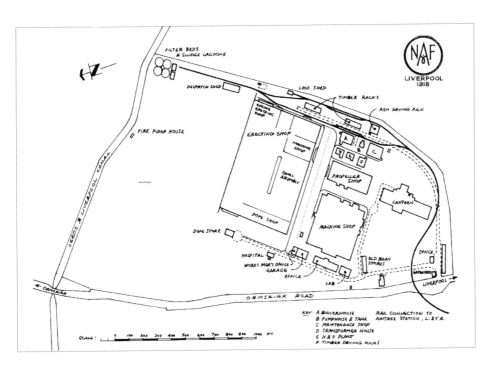

The plan of the National Aircraft Factory shows the layout of the 70-acre site, with the aerodrome laid out in the open space north of the factory buildings. (Based on plan in The National Archives, file ref. MUN 5/299)

The interior of the factory with female workers engaged in covering wings with fabric prior to 'doping'. Aircraft fuselages appear in the background. (Courtesy of University of Liverpool Library)

Another internal view, showing rows of aircraft fuselages awaiting assembly. (Courtesy of University of Liverpool Library)

aircraft were to be delivered to the 'Queensferry Aircraft Acceptance Park', located at RAF South Shotwick, later renamed RAF Sealand. Although it seems that many of the completed F.2Bs were packed and despatched by rail from the factory's spur line from the Lancashire & Yorkshire Railway, the delivery arrangement necessitated the preparation of an aerodrome at Aintree, and this was laid out immediately adjacent to, and to the north of, the factory itself. The alternative, of requisitioning part of Aintree Racecourse, was rejected in March 1918. The factory site was bounded by the Leeds and Liverpool Canal to the north, Ormskirk Road to the west and the Racecourse to the east.

The main contractor building the factory was the firm of Trollope & Colls, a building company that already had a branch at 17-25 Pleasant Street in the centre of Liverpool, at which (coincidentally) it had an Aeroplane Department making Avro 504 wings under contract to A.V. Roe & Co. Ltd. The contract arrangement with Cunard seems to have been an unhappy one - Trollope & Colls were also building other aircraft factories in Oldham, and were 'overstretched', while they were also angling to obtain sub-contract work from Cunard for their own Aeroplane Department. The Ministry of Munitions also caused problems for the work by making changes to the planned factory layout and showing indecision on the scope of work.

Cunard appointed Major C.K. Butler-Stoney of the Royal Flying Corps to be the manager of the Aeroplane Factory and by 14 March 1918 the Cunard Aeroplane Department moved to the Aintree factory site, resulting in the factory becoming a 'controlled establishment' under the Munitions of War Act on the following day. However, delivery of complete F.2Bs was due to begin in May, and it had become necessary to sub-contract much work in an attempt to meet the contractual deadline. By the beginning of February 1918, Cunard had placed an order for fifty F.2B fuselages with Rushworth & Dreaper, an organ maker in Liverpool, and soon afterwards ordered a further fifty from W. Watson & Co., a coachbuilder in Birkenhead. In each case these sub-contracts were priced at £3,250. It seems that the furniture firm of Waring & Gillow, which also had works in Liverpool, and was much involved in aeroplane manufacture during the First World War, was also a sub-contractor, since a photograph exists showing F.2B fuselage frames under construction in their Fleet Street works in Liverpool.

The Cunard Company continued to have problems with the bureaucrats in the Ministry of Munitions. The minutes of the Cunard Steamship Company's Board of Directors' meeting for 11 September 1918 records a decision that Sir Alfred Booth, chairman of the company, was to travel to London immediately after the meeting, together with his general manager, to meet Controller of National Aeroplane Factories Alexander Duckham. This arose because the Ministry of Munitions had asked Cunard to dismiss Captain Calder, the Superintendent of the Factory. Cunard took the line that they had a contract to manage the factory and were only prepared to do so on their own terms, without Ministry interference.

Consequently, at the end of work on 17 October 1918 the NAF was handed over to the Ministry of Munitions and all further Cunard involvement ceased. The war ended with the Armistice of 11 November, and the Ministry was left to deal with the cancellation of work, resulting in the last complete F.2B being handed over in January 1919 and the dispersal of the workforce. On 1 November 1918, a new contract had been placed for the factory to build 500 Sopwith Snipe fighters (serial numbers J4092 to J4591) at NAF No.3, but this order was cancelled later in the month following the declaration of the Armistice.

The factory continued to be owned by the Government and during January 1919 it was formally handed over to the Disposals Board and became No. 4 Aircraft Salvage Depot, storing engines, components and complete aircraft received from other sites all over the country. Some of these were refurbished and flown away in the hands of the Aircraft Disposal Company (Airdisco), a subsidiary of the Handley Page Aircraft Company which had been set up to sell surplus military aircraft and equipment at the end of the war. At some point, the Salvage Depot was closed and the buildings handed over to Airdisco. It is said that over 2,000 redundant aircraft, mostly dismantled, were stored in the factory, which might seem an incredible number, but would have only been a small fraction of the surplus aircraft available for disposal after the Armistice. Airdisco certainly handled thousands of aircraft and the Aintree depot was second in size to the company's main base at Waddon (Croydon), another former National Aircraft Factory. The Aintree site was certainly used for some civil aviation activities during the 1919-1926 period. The best known of these was a pioneering air service from Liverpool to the municipal aerodrome (Malone Air Park) at Belfast during 1924. This was flown by de Havilland D.H.50s of the de Havilland Aeroplane Hire Service, one of the pilots being Alan Cobham. The operating company was called Northern Air Lines, which hired the aircraft from de Havillands. Services commenced on 30 April 1924 with a flight from Belfast to Liverpool, piloted by Cobham. The tenuous nature of operations given the aviation infrastructure at the time is illustrated by the fact that the first flight in the opposite direction had to be abandoned at Southport due to bad weather. The main purpose of the service was to carry mail and newspapers between Liverpool and Belfast, with passengers carried at a fare of £3.0.0 if space was available. The DH50 could carry four passengers. The service was withdrawn on 2 June 1924, mainly due to the inadequacy of the aerodromes – the one at Belfast was never used again.

In October 1925, the factory site was purchased by the newly formed British Enka Company as their 'No.1 Factory' for the manufacture of rayon yarn. The adjacent aerodrome continued to be active until early 1926, at which point a 'Notice to Airmen' advised it could no longer be used because of building work on the site. This involved the construction of settling tanks for chemicals used in the British Enka production process, with the factory being opened in its new role during 1927.

British Enka was eventually taken over by the Courtaulds Group. The factory continued to operate until at least the mid-1960s but all the buildings on the site have since been demolished and replaced by modern buildings. One survival from the British Enka period is the name of 'Brenka Avenue' for a road at the south end of the site.

1
The Airport and
the Early Airlines

The First Steps

The events described in the Introduction resulted in Liverpool City Council calling for a detailed investigation to be made into the merits of establishing a municipal aerodrome. The results of this investigation were reported by the town clerk to the Finance & General Purposes Committee on 10 May 1929. Although the investigation had considered the merits of Aintree Racecourse and of Hooton Park, the report dealt in detail with only five possible sites for an aerodrome, four of them in the Speke Estate, with the fifth in Walton Hall Park to the north of the city. Two of the sites lay within the area of the now-closed north airfield, and a third within the present-day south airfield. A fourth possible area straddled what is now Woodend Avenue, Speke. One area in the centre of what later became the north airfield was recommended, the only reservation being that it was unsuitable for later development of a seaplane station because the nearest point on the river was too shallow for such a use. Walton Hall also met with some favour, because of the intended construction of the East Lancashire Road along its boundary, but it was rejected because the prevailing wind would blow the city smoke and fog over the site (much more of a problem in the days before the Clean Air Act). The Finance Committee recommended that an aerodrome be developed at the favoured site, and this was later accepted by the full council. Levelling work commenced about March 1930.

The completion of the first stage of work enabled the application for the first private-use aerodrome licence to be granted on 16 June 1930, in time for the arrival of an Armstrong-Whitworth Argosy airliner of Imperial Airways on that day, inaugurating a service from Croydon to Liverpool via Birmingham and Manchester. This experimental service was subsidised by Birmingham, Manchester and Liverpool Corporations, and was mainly intended to act as a feeder route to Imperial Airways' services from London. The flight operated three times per week in each direction (northbound flights on one day, southbound on the next), and was withdrawn on 20 September 1930 after 601 passengers had been carried. The service was judged to be a success, but in the event the stated intention to run the service in subsequent summer seasons was not fulfilled (probably because of the conditions of recession at

A map of the prospective airport sites under review in 1929, including: (1) Aintree racecourse; (2) Walton Hall Park (both north east of the city); (3) Hooton Park on the south bank of the Mersey; (4) the site chosen for the first stage of Speke Aerodrome; (5) another site, later incorporated into the airport as it expanded; (6) A third site, adjacent to Woodend Avenue and the later Ford factory, never developed; (7) a fourth site, considered 'too expensive to prepare' in 1929, but now the site of Liverpool Airport as it is today; (8) Liverpool Marine Airport, operated by the Mersey Docks & Harbour Board, 1928–40.

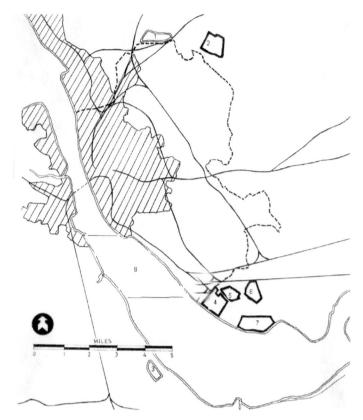

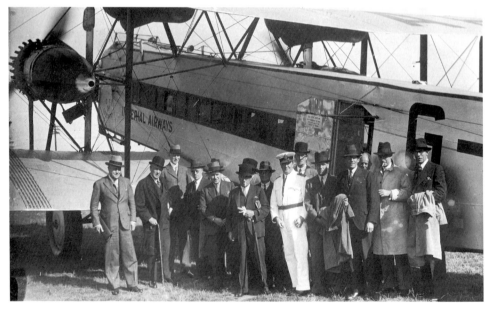

The Armstrong-Whitworth Argosy I G-AACI *City of Coventry* pictured at the inauguration of the Liverpool (Speke)–Manchester (Barton)–Birmingham (Castle Bromwich)–London (Croydon) service by Imperial Airways in June 1930. (Phil Butler collection)

the time). No more regular commercial services were operated until after Liverpool Airport was opened to public use on 1 July 1933. At the time of the 1930 services the longest grass runway was 800 yards in length, and the only aerodrome building was a wooden office on the north-east side of the landing ground.

During the period of the Imperial Airways experimental service, Sir Alan Cobham had been engaged to advise the corporation on further development of the airport, and his report was issued in February 1931. This recommended the construction of an airport building and two hangars adjacent to Sutton Grange, on the side of the north airfield nearest to Speke Hall. This was part of a detailed plan which would eventually include many other hangars and buildings, served by a new dual carriageway road, an airport hotel, and a seaplane base close to the later Liverpool Sailing Club slipway. This plan was initially authorised to proceed to its first stage, but was rescinded in April 1932 due to the financial stringency of the time, before any practical work had been done.

During 1931, therefore, the main activity at Speke was flying by the Liverpool & District Aero Club; although the club was still based at Hooton Park, the Speke aerodrome licence had been amended on 1 November 1930 to permit the club to make instructional flights from there. Towards the end of 1931 further levelling on the site was authorised on land between the original landing area and the river. In May 1932 the city council decided to proceed with development of the airfield, but on a more modest basis than the grandiose Cobham plan, by adapting the existing Chapel House Farm for aviation use – converting the farmhouse into a terminal building

A map showing the layout of the Cobham plan for the development of the airport. The building at top left is the Bryant & May match works, and the fields and farmyard to the right belong to Mount Pleasant Farm, where the 1938 terminal was later built. The Cobham plan was never started because of the financial constraints of the time.

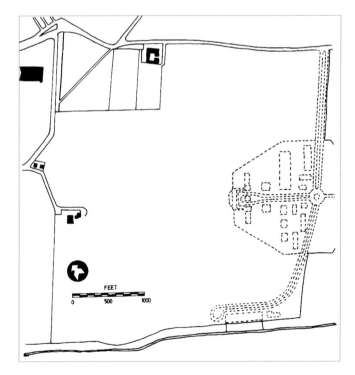

A 1931 view of the airfield, with the Chapel House Farm buildings intact. The airfield used in 1930 is the area above the roadway that extends to the right of the farm buildings. Just visible in the original print is a windsock at the end of the right-hand hedgerow in the top left of the photograph. (Phil Butler collection)

A view of the Imperial Airways Handley Page HP.42 *Hengist*, taken on the day of the Grand National race in 1932, when it brought in race-goers. The original wooden shed used as a terminal building is under the nose of the aircraft. (City of Liverpool, Phil Butler collection)

G-ABSI, an Airspeed Ferry of Alan Cobham's Flying Circus, which carried out pleasure flying in 1932 during a visit of the air display to Speke on 11 June. In the following year, Midland & Scottish Air Ferries used aircraft of the same type for services to Dublin and elsewhere. (Phil Butler collection)

and offices, and roofing over the farmyard to provide a hangar, with workshops in the surrounding farm buildings. While this development was in the planning stage, Captain Harold James Andrews had been appointed as airport manager on 6 July 1932.

This appointment was a fortunate one, for Captain Andrews was an energetic man with experience in many aspects of aviation, and he was to serve the city well in the years up to 1939. The arrival of the airport manager, who became a key figure in planning future developments, was a significant milestone in the development of the airport. It affirmed the city's commitment to the airport as a serious enterprise and for the first time provided a full-time professional co-ordinator for the whole project.

The Official Opening

A great deal of preparation went into the organisation of the flying programme to surround the official airport opening ceremony on 1 July 1933. The outcome left a lasting impression on the minds of those who witnessed it. The aim had been to produce the largest civil air display of the year as Liverpool took its place on the

A view taken in 1933, with the Chapel House Farm buildings converted and 'Liverpool' in a white circle in the middle of the main flying area. The windsock is still flying at the end of the hedge. (Phil Butler collection)

The Chapel House Farm area in 1933, showing the newly completed hangar and the farmhouse ready for use as a station building. (Phil Butler collection)

The Saunders-Roe Cloud amphibian G-ABXW *Cloud of Iona* shown at Speke on the day before the official opening display on 1 July 1933, where it provided pleasure flights. (FoLA/Alan Thelwell collection)

world's air map, with the finest civil aerodrome in the country, covering an area of 350 acres. Enthusiasm among the public had been steadily generated in the week beforehand by news of the cavalcade of aircraft due to attend. On the Friday before the event, the RAF rehearsed parts of their contribution to the display, and among the civilian contributors to the event the Duchess of Bedford's Fokker F.VIIA G-EBTS and Lord Malcolm Douglas-Hamilton's Saro Cloud amphibian G-ABXW displayed themselves, the Cloud taking off and landing on the Mersey as well as at Speke itself. At the end of the day, the RAF aircraft departed to Sealand to spend the night, before returning for the display proper.

The display itself included the Fairey Long-Range Monoplane (K1991), which had set a long-distance record earlier in the year by flying from Cranwell to Walvis Bay in South-West Africa, and the RAF contribution also included Hawker Demons of No.23 Squadron, Hawker Furies of No.25 Squadron and Avro Tutors of the Central Flying School. The airport was officially opened by Lord Londonderry, the Secretary of State for Air, who arrived in a Hawker Hart of No.24 Squadron, escorted by Bristol Bulldogs of No.29 Squadron.

There were varied contributions from civilian aircraft. As well as the large Fokker and the Saro Cloud already mentioned, pleasure flights were given by Dragon G-ACGU of Blackpool & West Coast Air Services, which also took part in a staged airliner departure (proper airline services did not start until the following Monday).

G-ACFF *Progress II* DH Fox Moth of Blackpool & West Coast Air Services, at Speke on the 1933 opening day. (Phil Butler collection)

The new 'Liverpool Airport' sign at the junction of Banks Lane and Speke Road. (FoLA/Alan Thelwell collection)

Left: Planning the opening display – air display consultant Frank Courtney, Group Captain Hunter (commander of the RAF contingent) and airport manager H.J. Andrews. (Phil Butler collection)

Below: Lord Londonderry making his speech at the opening ceremony. Also on the stand are Air Marshal Sir Robert Brooke-Popham, the Lord Mayor (Councillor Alfred Gates JP) and Frank Courtney. (FoLA/Alan Thelwell collection)

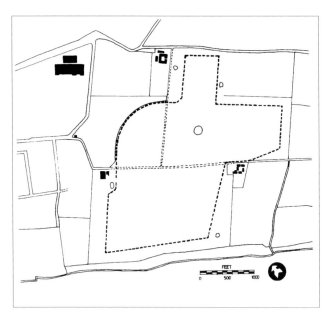

A map showing the airfield layout for the opening display in 1933.

Many private aircraft arrived, some taking part in a time of arrival competition, with prizes given for arriving at their pre-declared time. Other private aircraft took part in a Liverpool–Blackpool–Liverpool Air Race, the oldest competitor being a Bristol F.2B fighter of First World War vintage (which also won the race). Among the unusual civilian types in the display was a Cierva Autogiro, flown by R.A.C. Brie.

Early Days of the Airlines

The May 1932 decision to develop the airport included the intention to obtain a full public-use licence, to obtain customs facilities (a necessary pre-requisite to the title airport), and to provide permanent refuelling facilities, lack of which had previously caused some embarrassment. A tender for the construction of the first hangar (later known as No.50 Hangar) was accepted on 4 January 1933, and the various works which went ahead in parallel with this construction enabled the public-use licence to be issued on 10 June, to take effect from 16 June. Airline services commenced on 3 July 1933, with Fox Moths and a Dragon of Blackpool & West Coast Air Services flying to Blackpool (daily) and the Isle of Man (twice daily), a planned earlier start of 22 June having been postponed until after the display. A second company, Midland & Scottish Air Ferries Ltd, advertised a network of services to Dublin, Cork, Belfast via Blackpool and the Isle of Man via Rhyl, to start on 7 August. This company was based at Hooton Park, and in the event only one service via Speke was actually started, being a daily Hooton–Speke–Dublin (Baldonnel) flight, which ran from 14 August until 30 September, flown by Avro Ten G-ACGF or Airspeed Ferries G-ACBT and G-ACFB.

Late in 1933 the city council was approached by the Liverpool & District Aero Club with a request for permanent facilities to be provided for them at Speke. Since the lease on the club's Hooton premises was due to run out in July 1934, this was an urgent matter, and agreement was quickly reached. Loan sanction was received on 22 January 1934 for the construction of a clubhouse and hangar with separate gate and access road between the Chapel House Farm buildings and the river. The hangar became No.54 Hangar when the buildings were given numbers by the Air Ministry during the Second World War. The total cost of £7,870 was borne by the corporation, which then let the buildings to the Aero Club on a long lease from 1 August 1934. The Liverpool club grew strongly in the years up to 1939, particularly with the formation of the Civil Air Guard organisation in 1938. The CAG enabled its civilian members to receive training subsidised by the Air Ministry, in exchange for an undertaking to serve in time of war. It was not part of the RAF, Auxiliary Air Force or RAF Volunteer Reserve, but its members trained in local aero clubs such as the one at Speke.

In 1934, airline services began in earnest. On 6 April, the Prime Minister, Ramsey MacDonald, flew from Birmingham (Castle Bromwich) to Speke in the Avro 642 G-ACFV, which he later named *Marchioness of Londonderry*, and attended an inaugural dinner with the Air Minister and civic dignitaries from Glasgow, Belfast, Liverpool, Birmingham and the Isle of Man to celebrate the opening of Midland & Scottish Air Ferries' routes on 9 April. These comprised twice-daily flights on the routes London–Birmingham–Liverpool–Glasgow and Liverpool–Isle of Man–Belfast.

Inauguration of the Midland & Scottish Air Ferries internal air services, 6 April 1934. This event brought almost the whole MSAF fleet to Speke, with two Airspeed Ferries, three DH Dragons, four Fox Moths and two Avro Cadets lined up for inspection. (Phil Butler collection)

G-ACPX DH Dragon, of Railway Air Services, at Speke on the day of the inaugural Railway Air Services' flight on the Liverpool–Birmingham–Cardiff–Haldon–Plymouth route, 7 May 1934. (RAF Museum neg. P013339)

DH.60G Gipsy Moth G-AAIA pictured in front of the almost complete Liverpool Aero Club hangar at Speke in 1934. Part of the new clubhouse can be seen to the left. The Moth wears a 'Liver Bird' device on its rudder. The details of the colour scheme are not known, but later the club aircraft had yellow fuselages with registrations in blue. (Richard Riding)

Members of the Civil Air Guard being inspected at Speke in the summer of 1939. The Civil Air Guard was a voluntary organisation with branches attached to flying clubs all over the country, which enabled its members to receive subsidised pilot training. The CAG was subsidised by the Air Ministry, but was not part of the RAF or the RAF Volunteer Reserve. The aircraft in the background are Tiger Moths of the Liverpool & District Aero Club. (Phil Butler collection)

The Civil Air Guard building at its opening ceremony in 1939, with the Aero Club hangar in the background. The CAG building was used by various aero clubs after the war; the original Liverpool Aero Club building, located beyond the other end of the hangar, was by then in use by the Ministry of Civil Aviation. (Phil Butler collection)

Above: A Fox Moth of Midland & Scottish Air Ferries about to depart for Glasgow in 1934 with passengers Mr and Mrs J.L. Forrest. The ladder against the aircraft was no doubt used by an airport hand to reach the fuel tank on top of the wing centre-section – the pipe carrying the petrol from the tank to the aircraft's engine can be seen above the passengers' heads. (Mrs V.C. Forrest)

Below: G-ACFV Avro 642 of Midland & Scottish Air Ferries at Speke, 1934. Chapel House Farm is behind, with the dormer extension enabling the watch officer to view the airfield from the roof level. (Phil Butler collection)

Above: The inaugural KLM service to Amsterdam in May 1934. The aircraft is a Fokker F.XII. None of the worthies can be identified, apart from H.J. Andrews, who is to the left of the gentleman shaking hands with the KLM pilot.

Below: G-ACFC DH Fox Moth of Blackpool & West Coast Air Services in front of the Chapel House hangar in 1934, with the Chapel House itself behind the aircraft. This one was also named *Progress*, the name coming from a bus company that ran tours to Blackpool from places in Lancashire and Yorkshire, and which offered connections to B&WCAS flights. The Fox Moth colour scheme was black with white registration and titles. (Richard Riding)

Another view of a KLM Fokker F.XII (PH-AID) with the newly completed Liverpool Aero Club hangar (then called Hangar No.2), behind. The Fokker is parked in front of the Chapel House Farm.

Hillman Airways' Rapide G-ADAL, with a 'futuristic' Post Office vehicle (advertising Air Mail) at Speke in 1935, probably soon after Hillman had obtained an airmail contract from the Post Office.

The flight timings were arranged to provide connections at Liverpool with the planned KLM Liverpool–Hull–Amsterdam service, which in fact commenced on 1 June, to provide Belfast and Glasgow with continental links. However, these ambitious operations ceased on 14 July, because of pressure on the proprietor, John Sword, to concentrate on his other business interests (bus services in Scotland). A contributory factor was certainly that the 'London' terminal was at Romford (and later at Abridge), both of them far from the city or any connecting airlines services beyond London. The MSAF operation was in fact taken over by Hillman's Airways, another pioneer private airline, and their London (Stapleford)–Liverpool–Belfast service, operated once daily in each direction by DH Dragons, started on 16 July. The Isle of Man was omitted from the route because Hillman considered the aerodromes there to be unsuitable. The service was suspended temporarily in September, but restarted on 1 December following the award of a Post Office contract to Hillman to carry mail over the route. In the meantime, Blackpool & West Coast recommenced their Liverpool–Blackpool–Isle of Man services during May, which then ran summer and winter until taken over by Isle of Man Air Services during 1937.

On 7 May, Railway Air Services (RAS) had begun their first airline operation, operated on weekdays over the route Liverpool–Birmingham–Cardiff–Teignmouth–Plymouth, using Dragon G-ACPX. RAS was owned jointly by the four main railway companies, and over the next fourteen years it made a major contribution to the development of British internal airline services. In August RAS started a Glasgow–Belfast–Manchester–Birmingham–London route, but from 1 November the route transferred to Liverpool (omitting Birmingham and Manchester). As mentioned earlier, KLM had started the Liverpool–Hull–Amsterdam service, which was flown by three-engined Fokker F.XIIs every weekday until 6 October. This was the first service flown by a foreign airline to provincial points in the United Kingdom. KLM were allowed to carry domestic passengers on the Liverpool–Hull sector, and they offered connections at Amsterdam to Hamburg, Berlin, Copenhagen, Malmö and Rotterdam. Mail was carried on this service from 13 August 1934.

Development Begins – the Hangar and Station Building

The progress that had been made in 1934 changed the climate of caution which had previously caused the Cobham proposals to be deferred. On 2 May the city council authorised the despatch of a special sub-committee to visit the Continent to study facilities in use or planned at a number of airports, including Amsterdam and Hamburg, and on 4 July the council instructed its Land Steward and Surveyor to submit plans along the lines of the layout inspected at Hamburg. On the same date it was decided to close Bailey's Lane (which then formed the eastern boundary of the licensed airfield) to install boundary, obstruction and floodlighting at a cost of £6,500, to demolish Sutton Grange which still stood on the Speke Hall side of the airfield, and to take steps to control the erection of buildings near the airport which might cause hazards to air navigation.

PH-AKH, a Douglas DC-2 of KLM, photographed on 25 May 1935 when this aircraft visited on a demonstration flight, in connection with an Empire Air Day display, also attended by Alan Cobham's Air Circus.

G-ACVZ DH.86 *Jupiter* of Railway Air Services at Speke in 1935. Note the dormer watch office now sports the letter C (for 'control') and there is now a railing above the window to provide an even higher observation level! (RAF Museum P013344)

The futuristic-looking 'airport limousine', registration number AKC 800, used to transport airline passengers from the city centre. This was purchased at a cost of £600 (quite a sum for a road vehicle in 1935). (Phil Butler collection)

The nose of a Blackpool & West Coast Air Services DH.86, with a Shell-BP fuel bowser and the original hangar behind. This photograph was probably taken early in 1936. (Phil Butler collection)

Above: A busy scene outside the Chapel House, probably the day of the Aintree Grand National Race in 1936. Note the new three-wheeled Thompson Brothers' petrol bowser bought by the corporation in March 1936. A similar vehicle was used by Shell at Speke until the 1950s. The aircraft visible include an Avro Cadet of the Lancashire Aero Club (G-ACMG), Rapides G-ACTT and G-ACYR, three Spartan Cruisers, an Airspeed Envoy, a GAL Monospar, a Miles Hawk, a Miles Falcon and a Dragon.

Opposite above: The steelwork for the new hangar being erected, probably taken during 1936. (Phil Butler collection)

Opposite below: A shot taken from the Chapel House building in 1936, showing Rapides G-ACPP and G-ACPR of Railway Air Services, DH86 G-ADVJ *Ronaldsway* and Dragon G-ADCP of Blackpool & West Coast Air Services, and Rapide G-ADAH and Spartan Cruiser G-ACVT of British Airways, all awaiting passengers.

Overleaf above: The opening ceremony for the new hangar and control tower in June 1937, with Lord Derby preparing to make his speech from a dais in the doorway of the hangar. This may have been the point at which the hangar annexe came into use as a temporary terminal. The semi-circular office at the south end of the annexe (just visible adjacent to the folding door at the left) was also used as a temporary watch office before the control tower itself came into use. (Phil Butler collection)

Overleaf below: A view from the top of the Chapel House Farm taken in 1937, showing a de Havilland DH.86 Express (G-ADVK of West Coast Air Services), the new Hangar D (later No.1), and the new control tower. The number of ruts in the grass show that the Chapel House Farm area was still in use, but by mid-1937 the terminal was moved to the side annexe of the new hangar. (Phil Butler collection)

Work proceeded swiftly and on 3 October plans for the first stage of the development were approved – namely the construction of what is now generally known as Hangar No.1, and of the control tower which still forms the central point of the terminal building on the now-disused north airfield. Two days later, application was made for sanction to install a radio approach beacon of the type used at Amsterdam Airport. Sanction for this was refused for some time, but was obtained in March 1935.

Concurrent with all this activity, many other negotiations went on to attract aeronautical industries to the Speke Estate, and to involve Liverpool Airport in possible transatlantic air services. At one point negotiations were almost completed to set up the British Bellanca Aircraft Company in the Speke Estate, this being a British subsidiary of the Bellanca Aircraft Corporation of New Castle, Delaware, at that time a prominent manufacturer of small commercial aircraft in the USA, but in the end these came to nothing. Various discussions were held with possible operators of transatlantic flying-boat services, to be fed by internal and continental airlines connecting with them at Speke. One interesting proposal was for a Stockholm–Liverpool–New York airship service operated by a Zeppelin to be purchased by a consortium of Scandinavian shipowners. Press statements talk of the Zeppelin being ordered, but no more came of the proposal.

During the year work progressed on the planned development. Tenders were accepted totalling £47,560 for construction of the large hangar and for the foundations of the control tower, and consent was obtained for spending £38,600 on levelling, drainage works and on removing the roadway of Bailey's Lane. By the end of 1936, work was well advanced on the main hangar (then called Hangar D, but more familiar to the present-day reader as No.1), and on the control tower, while in September loan sanction had been received for part of the work on the foundations and cellars for the new station building to be constructed around the tower. Work on the building itself was held up pending resolution of an argument with the Air Ministry Civil Aviation Department about the shape of the building, which had been designed (and was later built) in the concave shape we know today, instead of the convex shape favoured by the Air Ministry. Until the argument was settled, loan consent for part of the money required was withheld.

The main hangar and the control tower were opened on 11 June 1937, at a ceremony presided over by Lord Derby. Pending completion of the new station building, part of the hangar and the office annexe on the landward side of the hangar were in use as a temporary terminal. During this period aircraft were parked in three sides of the hangar, the space on the landward side of the building being used as a customs area. Shortly after this ceremony (and a report to a meeting of the city council on 7 July), consent was received to borrow £80,500 to complete the terminal building. A compromise had been reached on the shape of the building: consent was given for the concave plan provided that the next phase of construction, when traffic growth warranted an extension, should be a separate low circular building in front of the existing one, connected to it by underground passages (comparable to the 'beehive' at pre-war Gatwick). The Air Ministry considered this layout was essential to prevent congestion of parked aircraft.

Airline Operations Expand

In 1935, the pattern of summer services was similar to that of the previous year. The KLM service restarted on 30 April, only to terminate prematurely on 26 July due to a shortage of pilots. The Blackpool & West Coast Isle of Man operations had run throughout the winter, partly as a result of a Post Office contract to carry mail, but from 31 May a competitive RAS service was flown three times daily. The RAS west and south of England service restarted on 27 May, this time twice-daily with DH Rapides. In 1935 the routing was Liverpool–Birmingham–Bristol–Southampton–Portsmouth–Shoreham; connecting flights at Birmingham maintained the link to Cardiff, Teignmouth and Plymouth. On 6 June Hillman's Airways started a Liverpool–Manchester–Hull service, whil on the 18th United Airways Ltd became a third operator on the Liverpool–Blackpool–Isle of Man route. On 1 August Crilly Airways started a twice-daily Liverpool–Leicester service, which connected with Isle of Man and Belfast flights at Speke and with Norwich, Nottingham, Northampton and Bristol services at Leicester. On 1 November, United Airways gained the Liverpool–Isle of Man mail contract and then commenced direct services (omitting the Blackpool stop). The level of traffic now entailed about eighty air-transport movements on a summer's day, amply justifying the city's faith in its airport development plans.

By the beginning of 1936 a new airline name appeared, that of British Airways Ltd. This was a private company set up by the Whitehall Securities group, with the aim of establishing a private enterprise alternative to the state-owned Imperial Airways. The new company incorporated Hillman's Airways and United Airways, whose Liverpool operations continued under the new name. The Liverpool–Manchester–Hull route had been abandoned before the end of 1935, so the 1936 route structure comprised twice-daily Liverpool–Belfast–Glasgow services (flown Mondays–Saturdays), once-daily Liverpool–Blackpool flights (also Monday–Saturday), and Liverpool–Blackpool–Isle of Man (twice on Sundays and three times on other days). On 1 July, Northern & Scottish Airways (which had earlier in the year gained the Isle of Man–Liverpool mail contract) took over all the British Airways' Irish Sea routes, having on that day become a wholly owned subsidiary of British Airways. The N&SA fleet consisted of four Rapides and five Spartan Cruisers. On the same day KLM restarted their Amsterdam service, this time via Doncaster instead of Hull, and operating in conjunction with British Continental Airways, another British Airways' subsidiary. Blackpool & West Coast Air Services continued to fly Liverpool–Isle of Man services each weekday, with additional twice-daily operations over the Manchester–Liverpool–Blackpool–Isle of Man route. From 14 September to 24 October Aer Lingus and Blackpool & West Coast Air Services operated Liverpool–Dublin services (using the name 'Irish Sea Airway'), the first flight being made by the Aer Lingus Dragon EI-ABI. The Crilly Airways Leicester–Liverpool service continued to fly twice daily until October, when the airline closed down following the appointment of a receiver on 9 September. Railway Air Services continued to be the largest operator with flights as follows:

The temporary watch office at the end of the new hangar, with telephones and meteorological briefing information visible in the original print. This shot was taken in 1939, after the control tower itself was in operation (although the roads around the landside of the building in the background are still not complete). (Phil Butler collection)

A view inside Hangar D, showing a Blackpool & West Coast Air Services DH.86, G-AENR, dwarfed by the structure. (Phil Butler collection)

The Airspeed Envoy G-AEXX of the King's Flight at Speke on an unknown date (but probably 1937). It is parked between the new hangar and Speke Road, this area being reserved for foreign arrivals and departures and other special flights. Note the railway freight sheds behind the aircraft which were immediately opposite the later entrance road for the 1938 terminal building.

Liverpool–Isle of Man, Manchester–Liverpool–Isle of Man, Leeds–Manchester–Liverpool–Isle of Man (all daily), and Manchester–Liverpool–Blackpool–Isle of Man (twice daily), all of which operated under the name 'The Manx Airway', Manchester–Liverpool–Stoke–Birmingham–Gloucester–Bristol–Southampton–Ryde–Brighton (May–September, daily on weekdays, with additional services on Mondays, Tuesdays, Fridays and Saturdays) and London–Birmingham–Stoke–Liverpool–Belfast–Glasgow (daily on weekdays).

The pattern of operations described for 1936 continued with few changes in the following three years up to the outbreak of the Second World War. From 27 September 1937, Isle of Man Air Services took over the Isle of Man routes from Railway Air Services, still under the name of the 'Manx Airway'. Isle of Man Air Services had been in existence since 1935, but during September 1937 it was reorganised and became jointly owned by Olley Air Service, the Isle of Man Steam Packet Co. Ltd and the London, Midland and Scottish Railway. In May 1939, the original RAS route to the Isle of Wight via Birmingham, Bristol and Southampton was taken over by Great Western and Southern Air Lines (owned by the two railway companies). The Amsterdam service continued, but was run solely by KLM after the start of the 1937 timetable; the service omitted Doncaster after 1937, routing via Manchester instead after the opening of Ringway Airport in 1938. The old Fokker F.XIIs had by then given way to Douglas DC-2s, with some Lockheed 14s used in 1938 and Douglas DC-3s appearing in 1939.

The operation pattern changed abruptly at the end of August 1939, when civilian flights were suspended on the imminent outbreak of war. (Internal airline flights were resumed after a few weeks.)

Above: A panoramic shot taken in April 1939, showing Hangar D, the now-complete terminal (with the Mount Pleasant Farm building demolished), and the 'fog line' laid out on the airfield. This was in white along the line of the Lorenz radio beam approach system that had been installed in 1937 (the fog line itself was a 1939 innovation). The transverse bars were to show 'distance gone' from the airfield boundary, and the X markings to tell the pilot he was near the end of the available run. (Liverpool Record Office)

Below: A map dated 1939 showing the airport's location and the planned Speke Estate, although the estate layout shown was not exactly what was built!

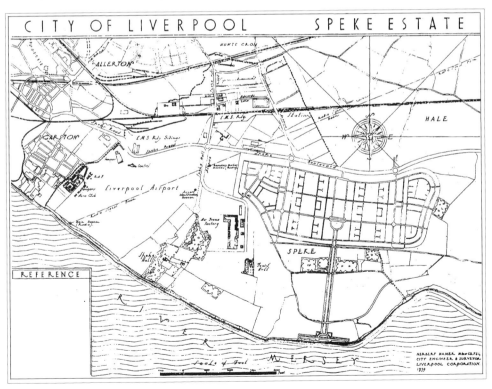

Left: The control tower in early 1938, showing steelwork for the terminal building being erected. DH Rapide G-AEAK of Railway Air Services is in the foreground. The annexe to Hangar D was then in use as the terminal building. Behind the terminal and tower is Mount Pleasant Farm (also known as Marsh Farm – formerly owned by a Mr Marsh), where H.J. Andrews and his family lived until their flat in the terminal building was completed. (Phil Butler collection)

Below: The completed terminal building in 1938, with de Havilland Express *Venus* (G-AEWR) of Railway Air Services in the foreground. (Phil Butler collection)

Above: Another view of *Venus*, possibly taken on the same occasion as the previous shot. Visible (above the heads of the ground crew) is one of the canvas-covered Bessoneau hangars of the Auxiliary Air Force squadron. (Phil Butler collection)

Below: The newly complete station building, seen in late 1938, with work on the concrete apron still to be completed. Note there is a watch officer with an Aldis lamp on duty in the top level of the control tower. (Phil Butler collection)

Above: A view inside the control tower in 1938, showing a watch officer in his white overalls, and the pneumatic tubes used for delivering messages from the lower floors of the building. (Phil Butler collection)

Below: Another view inside the control tower. The layout to the left of the watch officer is a mimic of the aerodrome, with switches for the large floodlights then used to illuminate the grass landing area at night. The large round dial appears to be a wind direction indicator. (Phil Butler collection)

2

Preparations for War

Auxiliary Air Force

Apart from the airline operations, the most significant events of the year 1936 for Liverpool Airport were the formation of No.611 (West Lancashire) Squadron of the Auxiliary Air Force, which was to be based at Speke, and the continuing work on the new hangar and control tower.

No.611 Squadron was formed at Hendon on 10 February 1936 on a name only basis, five days after Liverpool City Council had granted a tenancy to the Air Ministry of 5 acres of land, on which the tenant was to construct roadways and erect temporary buildings. The squadron was a unit of the Auxiliary Air Force, a reserve organisation similar to the Territorial Army. Its squadrons had a small nucleus of regular personnel who were mainly concerned with administration and aircraft maintenance, but the majority of the officers and men were recruited from geographical areas local to the unit and trained at weekends and during a two-week annual training camp. (The Auxiliary Air Force only became the Royal Auxiliary Air Force after the war.)

The intended role of the new squadron was as day bombers, using single-engined Hawker Hart biplanes; this role was maintained until 1 January 1939, when the squadron was reclassified as a fighter unit. After a short period based in St George's Buildings, the local Territorial Army headquarters, during which time its first commanding officer, Squadron Leader G.L. Pilkington, was commissioned, the squadron took over its offices, barrack huts and the first of two Bessoneau canvas hangars on 1 May 1936, moving in on 6 May. On 18 and 19 May its first three Avro Tutor training aircraft arrived, followed on 4 June by its first Hawker Hart. During the pre-war period, auxiliary squadrons often trained their own pilots from scratch – hence the Tutors, which remained with the Squadron Training Flight throughout its time at Speke. By the end of 1936 the squadron had a strength of eleven officers and fifty-two men and had flown 327 hours. During 1936 the city council also tendered to the Air Ministry for the establishment of an RAF Volunteer Reserve flying training school at Speke, but Liverpool's tender was initially unsuccessful. During this period many such schools were being established at civilian aerodromes, being run by civilian contractors on behalf of the Air Ministry.

Above: K6474, the Hawker Hart (Trainer) of No.611 (West Lancashire) Squadron, at Speke in 1937. The 611 Squadron number is painted below the cockpit, as was the practice at that time. 611 was 'Liverpool's own', but it was not called the City of Liverpool Squadron, perhaps because its first commanding officer, Squadron Leader Geoffrey Langton Pilkington of glassworks fame, came from St Helens. (Aldon Ferguson)

Opposite above: An aerial view of RAF Speke, showing the Auxiliary Air Force site. This was probably taken in 1937, since the Chapel House was still in use – there are two DH.86s parked in front of it. Also shown is part of the Liverpool Aero Club hangar, at the top of the picture, and the two AAF canvas hangars within the AAF site. (Aldon Ferguson)

Opposite below: Tom Campbell Black's Mew Gull G-AEKL in the Chapel House hangar after its accident on 19 September 1936. The Mew Gull had come to Speke to be named *Miss Liverpool*. It was being sponsored by the Moores family (of Littlewoods) as an entry in the 1936 London–Johannesburg Air Race, but was hit by a landing Hawker Hart as Campbell Black was preparing to take off after the ceremony. (H. Smith)

Another view of a Hawker Hart. (It is probably also the Hart (T) K6474, since this version had the distinctive exhaust manifold angled to disperse below the lower wing.) The squadron had only one dual-control Hart (T), but eight Hart bombers. In the background, to the left, is a corner of the Chapel House hangar, to the right a Bessoneau hangar. (Aldon Ferguson)

A tragic event was the death of the well-known airman Tom Campbell Black on 19 September 1936. Campbell Black was best known for his winning flight from England to Australia in the 1934 Air Race, piloting the DH.88 Comet racer G-ACSS *Grosvenor House*. In 1936, another long-distance race had been announced, from England to Johannesburg, and Campbell Black had entered for it, sponsored by John Moores (of Littlewoods), flying a Percival Mew Gull, G-AEKL. After a ceremony at the airport to name the aircraft *Miss Liverpool*, Campbell Black was waiting to take off when a Hawker Hart bomber, K3044 of No.611 Squadron, hit his aircraft on landing, and Campbell Black died of his injuries.

During April 1938, the original Hawker Hart light bombers began to be replaced by the slightly updated Hawker Hind. These remained in service until after No.611 Squadron was redesignated as a day-fighter squadron early in 1939. In May 1939, the first six Supermarine Spitfire Is arrived, together with two Fairey Battle light bombers. The Battles were dual-control aircraft, intended to introduce the pilots to the mysteries of retractable undercarriages. The Battles remained with the unit as conversion aircraft until after the squadron was embodied into the regular Royal Air Force in August with the impending threat of war. The embodiment occurred while the squadron was holding its annual camp at Duxford, and the Spitfires and the main strength of its personnel remained there, only a few of the training-flight aircraft and some of the surplus personnel returning to Liverpool.

Royal Air Force Station Speke was formed on 24 August 1939 from the surplus personnel of No.611 Squadron not immediately required for war service on that unit. (Auxiliary units had a large complement of part-time people to keep the unit ticking over in peacetime – when these people became full-time on mobilisation the units were over-strength.)

Shadow Factory

While the station-building developments were taking place and being argued about, a most important event had taken place in January 1937. At that time rearmament against the threat of Nazi Germany was getting into its stride, and new aircraft factories were being built. Many of these were managed by motor or electrical companies on behalf of the government, because the resources of the existing air-craft companies were too thinly stretched to cope. The theory was that these shadow factories would duplicate the production of existing established aircraft types. Early in January it was announced that a factory to be managed by the Rootes motor group at White Waltham in Berkshire was to be cancelled and moved to a depressed area. Although several attempts were made by other local authorities, especially in the north of England, to secure the factory, the Liverpool bid was successful, not only because of the existing airfield and the acknowledged depressed-area status, but because of the city's completed plans to build housing in the Speke Estate, adjacent to the proposed factory. Air Ministry officials visited the site on 27 January and the agreed terms for the lease of 97.23 acres of land across Speke Hall Avenue from the airport boundary were approved by a special meeting of the city council on 12 February. On 15 February, Sir Thomas White and the Lord Mayor of Liverpool joined in a ceremony to cut the first sod at the site. (Sir Thomas White was chairman of the Speke Estate Sub-Committee and a leading figure in promoting the develop-ment of the airport.)

The very first Bristol Blenheim Mark I aircraft from the Rootes' production line at Speke, serial number L8362, pictured in October 1938. This aircraft went to No.84 Squadron RAF in Iraq. (Museum of British Road Transport, Rootes archive)

The Liverpool Aero Club building after it had been hit by a taxiing Fairey Battle of the AAF Squadron. This must have been in 1939. (Phil Butler collection)

A line of Blenheim Is awaiting delivery shortly before the war, photographed from the roof of the Rootes flight shed. (via George Jones)

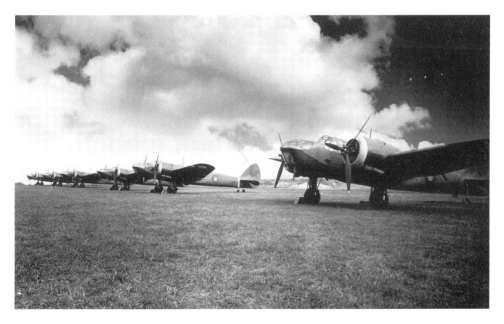

A line-up of Bristol Blenheim Mark IV aircraft (including L8864 and L8872), awaiting delivery in October 1939, after the outbreak of war. These were the 'long-nose' Blenheim. Note the aircraft tails strapped down to concrete blocks set in the ground, to prevent the aircraft nosing over while the engines were tested at full power. This photograph appears to have been taken on the airfield rather than within the Rootes site. (Museum of British Road Transport, Rootes archive)

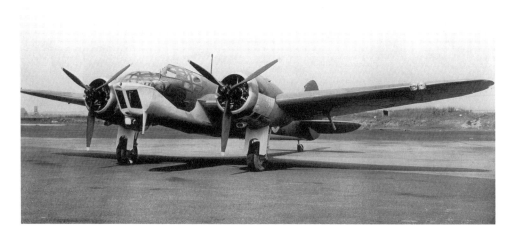

Bristol 'long-nose' Blenheim IV V6459, photographed on the Rootes site in April 1941. This aircraft had a short life, being destroyed in a flying accident at the main Blenheim training unit (No.54 OTU) on 12 June 1941, having flown fewer than twenty-one hours since new. (Museum of British Road Transport, Rootes archive)

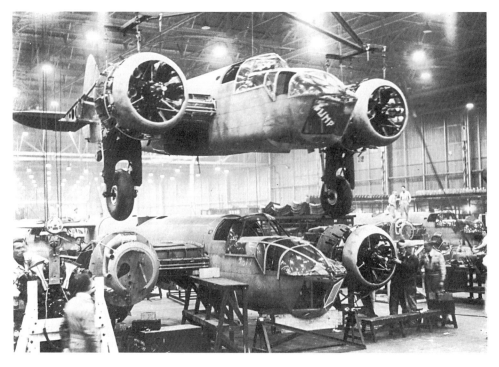

A view inside the Rootes factory, showing Blenheim IVs on the production line in 1940. (Phil Butler collection)

The Blenheim production lines inside the Rootes' factory during 1939. (Phil Butler collection)

Bristol Blenheim V (also known as the Bristol Bisley) prototype DJ702, photographed on Rootes' compass base in August 1941. This was the first of fifty-two built at Speke, before Blenheim V production was transferred to Rootes' Blythe Bridge factory. (Museum of British Road Transport, Rootes archive)

The factory was designed for the complete production of aircraft, from the receipt of raw material at one end to the despatch of complete aircraft at the other. As originally built during 1937, it was 1,440ft long and 400ft wide, with the height of the roof sections increasing in steps from 20ft to 30ft and 40ft. Rootes Securities Ltd had undertaken to produce the Bristol Blenheim Mk I bomber as a shadow for the Bristol Aeroplane Company, and Rootes' planning staff had been working at Bristol on preparation work for several months before the Speke site had even been chosen. Nevertheless the factory was planned such that larger aircraft than the Blenheim could be accommodated, and the Air Ministry for some time held an option on a further 60 acres of land, between the Rootes factory and the River Mersey, to enable factory extensions and slipways for flying boats to be built, for marine aircraft production. (This land included a significant proportion of the current south airfield.)

While the main factory was under construction, Rootes rented another factory in Edwards Lane, Speke, in order to train key staff members and to store such machine tools as arrived ahead of the completion of the main factory. Work had started on the receiving bay end of the main factory first, so that, as parts of that building were completed, production of aircraft components could start at once. This enabled the machine shop to start operating in September 1937, and the press shop in October. Sub-assembly of aircraft parts started in February 1938, and main assembly during the following month. The first main assembly of wings to forward and rear fuselages took place in June 1938, with the first Blenheim I, L8362, being flown away on delivery in October.

By the outbreak of war in September 1939, 250 Blenheim Is had been built, by which time production had just changed over to the long-nose Blenheim Mk IV. The factory had originally been required to build ten Blenheims per week. This had been increased to fifteen aircraft per week by the introduction of night-shift working, and then thirty per week, which required the first factory extensions (for additional machine shops). Shortly afterwards, the Air Ministry decided that a third of all work should be subcontracted in order to reduce the concentration of production in the relatively small number of easily targeted factories. This decision meant that the required production rate could be met without further extensions to the main factory. The initial contract had been for 600 Blenheims, with the balance of 350 (after completion of 250 Mk I aircraft) now being of the Mk IV version. Further contracts were placed in 1939, the main one on 6 June for a further 250 Blenheim IVs, with the others being for Blenheim spare parts and modification kits. The additional Blenheim IV contract was eventually extended several times to add further quantities of Blenheim Mk IV and V aircraft, of which more below. (Further details of the aircraft built appear in Appendix 2.)

Meanwhile, in February 1939, Rootes had been asked to plan for the production of the Short Stirling four-engined bomber. The plans envisaged building six Stirlings per month in addition to maintaining the planned rate of Blenheim manufacture, with the draft contract actually mentioning a total of 420 aircraft. This work really did require factory extensions, and resulted in the widening of those sections of

An early Halifax II from the Rootes production line, serial number DG235, photographed outside the Speke factory in September 1942. The Mk II & V aircraft had Rolls-Royce Merlin engines. (IWM ATP 10962B)

The very last Halifax A Mk VII from the Rootes production line, serial number NA468, surrounded by members of the workforce in July 1945. The propellers have still to be fitted, but otherwise the aircraft is complete. The later Mk III and Mk VII Halifaxes had Bristol Hercules radial engines. (David Smith)

One of the later Halifax III bombers, with Bristol Hercules radial engines, outside the Rootes flight shed with a large crowd of Rootes employees. (Colin Schroeder)

the factory that had not already been extended, so that almost the whole length of No.1 Factory became 600ft wide. The original Edwards Lane training centre then became No.2 Factory; a building within the Liverpool Corporation power station site at Lister Drive, Tuebrook, became No.3 Factory (intended for Stirling fuselage assembly); No.4 was a second works in Edwards Lane; and Nos 5/1 and 5/2 were in Widnes New Road (more familiar to most people as the Metal Box works). Widnes New Road was later renamed Speke Road. Plans for Stirling work were well advanced by May 1940 (with fuselage assembly under way), when the contract was cancelled. At that point priority was given to production of established types, so that Rootes' jigs and tools went to other Stirling production lines in a more advanced state (Shorts and Harland at Belfast, and Austin at Longbridge), while all drawings went to Canada where production was planned by Canadian Associated Aircraft. At about the same time, Blenheim production being undertaken by A.V. Roe at Manchester was cancelled, with their commitments transferred to Rootes. Also, Rootes was given a new contract to build two prototypes of the Bristol Bisley, a Blenheim development. This move provoked a furious reaction from the Bristol Aeroplane Co., who thought it was their job to produce prototypes. (Shadow factories were strictly banned from building prototypes, or carrying out any other work that would establish them as post-war aircraft manufacturers.) The Rootes contract was then put in abeyance, while a new contract for prototypes was placed with Bristol, but was later reinstated so that both companies made two prototypes. The No.1 Factory extensions were turned over for use as a service centre for the Bristol Blenheim, many hundreds of which arrived during the rest of 1940 and the first half of 1941 for modification work. This work was mainly 'tropicalisation' prior to service overseas. Rootes were also tasked to break down crashed Blenheims to recover materials and usable spare parts, and to support this task four Bellman hangars were erected on the west side of the factory site, coming into use in August 1940.

Later in 1940, the factory was again chosen to build a four-engined bomber – this time the Handley Page Halifax. By this time, it had already been planned to change Blenheim production from the Mk IV to the Mk V in August 1941 (the Mk V being the production version of the Bisley prototypes which had yet to fly; the Bisleys were being built in an experimental department at No.3 Factory). The initial plan was to build thirty-two Halifaxes per month, while maintaining production of twenty Blenheim Vs per month. While this was being investigated, the target was raised to forty Halifaxes and thirty-five Blenheims per month, which was beyond the factory's capacity. At this point, further production dispersal was being carried out, so that a No.6 Factory was being set up at Burtonwood to carry out some fuselage assembly, a No.7 Factory in Edwards Lane was coming into use as a store, and Nos 8 and 9 Factories were being brought into use. No.8 was at Meir aerodrome, Stoke-on-Trent, with No.9 at RAF Shawbury – their function was to provide dispersed final assembly and flight sheds for aircraft made from No.1 Factory assemblies.

No.8 Factory consisted of three Bellman hangars at Meir, and No.9 of two permanent hangars at Shawbury. Rootes proposed that Blenheim V production should transfer to an incomplete shadow factory under construction at Blythe Bridge (on the west side of Meir airfield), while the Speke No.1 Factory and its supporting facilities concentrated on the Halifax. The Blenheim service centre transferred to Meir in summer 1941, while Blenheim V production started in parallel at Speke and Blythe Bridge (the latter becoming No.10 Factory). The prototype Blenheim Vs and fifty production aircraft were built at Speke between September and December 1941, before the first Halifax flew in March 1942. A total of 1,070 Halifaxes of successive marks flew from Speke, while contracts for a further 620 were cancelled before the end of the war. The final production target was sixty Halifaxes per month. The last Halifax, a Mk VII airborne forces transport, flew on 9 July 1945. With the last Halifax, aircraft production ceased, and the factory was handed over to the Dunlop Rubber Company for the post-war production of tyres, industrial conveyor belts and other products.

3

Wartime Requisition

Lockheed Aircraft Corporation – British Reassembly Division

This operation was originally set up solely to reassemble Lockheed Hudsons after delivery by sea from California. The first contract for 200 aircraft had been placed in 1938, and the operation of what became the Lockheed British Reassembly Division began on 15 February 1939, when space was taken over in No.1 Hangar to assemble these aircraft. The operation very quickly grew in scale, such that on 22 February application was made to build a 'temporary' Bellman hangar alongside the main one. This hangar later became No.5 (most recently used by Deltair). On 27 June application was made for a second Bellman; when it was found there was not enough room to build this alongside No.5, it was positioned further along Banks Road and became the one used for many years by Keenair. At a later date a further Bellman was erected alongside this, nearer to No.1, this being the one latterly used by Vernair, and then by Cheshire Air Training School. Finally, another steel hangar (No.6), this time of the Ministry of Aircraft Production A1 type, was built between No.1 Hangar and Speke Road. Lockheed also used the corporation's permanent Lamella hangar (later known as No.2 Hangar) which was built in 1939 at Air Ministry expense, being originally intended for use by an RAFVR elementary and reserve flying training school (No.55 E&RFTS) that was cancelled at the outbreak of war. This was usually called the Douglas Hangar during the Lockheed time, since it was used for work on Douglas Bostons, while No.1 became the Lockheed Hangar.

Although initially set up solely to service the Hudson contract, Lockheed's organisation was the obvious candidate to provide a similar service for other US aircraft firms whose products were being shipped to the UK. This was particularly so because, whereas nowadays the British, American and Canadian aircraft industries have common standards for tooling (using common screw threads for example), this was not the case in 1939. An American aircraft on a British airfield would very soon be quite useless, because even the most elementary servicing required a completely different range of tools and spare parts. During the early months of 1940 the British government asked Lockheed to also handle the Douglas Boston; Lockheed agreed and this set the scene for a myriad of other types. Although Speke remained the headquarters for these activities, Lockheed set up operations in Scotland and Northern Ireland and because many of the surviving records do not differentiate between locations, it is often difficult to establish which activities took place at Speke and which elsewhere. In 1939, 141 Hudsons were assembled, the first two being delivered to Martlesham Heath on 3 April. Later on, aircraft of Hudson size were flown across the Atlantic, but in 1939 transatlantic flying was in its infancy and the risks were thought too great. After many preparations such as building airfields, weather stations and other new facilities, the first batch of Hudsons to be air-ferried flew from Gander to Aldergrove in November 1940. This batch of Hudsons duly landed at Speke on 12 November for post-delivery checks before entering RAF service. Thereafter valuable shipping space was reserved for single-engined aircraft and some of the shorter-range twin-engined types, but Lockheed continued to carry out servicing, modification and repair work on types which were delivered by air – particularly on Lockheed designs in general, but also on Douglas Bostons and the four-engined Consolidated Liberators.

Lockheed Hudson N7205 at Speke in March 1939, outside the main hangar. This was the first of the many Hudsons to be assembled by the Lockheed unit, having been shipped to Liverpool during the previous month. As seen here it has a mock-up of the dorsal gun turret. The gun turrets were fitted after the aircraft arrived in England, where these items were made by Boulton Paul Aircraft at Wolverhampton. (ATP 10125)

A Bellman 'temporary' hangar being erected at Speke in 1939, with houses in Banks Road and the Bryant & May match works in the background. This temporary hangar lasted for sixty years, the last occupants being a general aviation company called Deltair. The corner of the main large hangar must be just out of sight to the left. The hangar was erected for Lockheed to assemble Hudsons arriving from America. (Phil Butler collection)

A tanker carrying Lockheed P-38 Lightnings as deck cargo in the Mersey in February 1943. Birkenhead Town Hall and the air vents for the Mersey Tunnel are in the background. (David Smith)

Right: North American
P-51 Mustangs on the
luggage boat *Oxton* after
unloading from the deck
of a transport in the
Mersey. They are about
to be set down on the
Princes Landing Stage.
(Courtesy of the National
Museums in Liverpool
(Merseyside Maritime
Museum))

Below: Republic
Thunderbolts for the
USAAF being unloaded
from the *Oxton* on to the
Princes Landing Stage,
with an armed troopship
alongside the stage.
(Courtesy of the National
Museums in Liverpool
(Merseyside Maritime
Museum))

Republic P-47 Thunderbolts being transported from the Princes Landing Stage up the floating roadway at the Pier Head. These were brought ashore and taken to Speke or Burtonwood for assembly and removal of the protective treatment against salt–water corrosion, before delivery to the USAAF. (Courtesy of the National Museums in Liverpool (Merseyside Maritime Museum))

North American P-51 Mustangs being towed along Allerton Road towards Speke Airport in June 1944. The Plaza cinema is still there but is now a shopping centre. (Phil Butler collection)

Chance Vought Kingfisher FN656 for the Fleet Air Arm at Speke in April 1942, after assembly by Lockheed. Kingfishers were usually seen on floats, being operated from armed merchant cruisers as observation aircraft in the South Atlantic or Indian Ocean. (ATP 10847E)

Lockheed Ventura FN957 at the Lockheed unit for post-delivery checks in May 1943. After trials in England at Defford and Boscombe Down, this aircraft went to the South African Air Force, based at Gibraltar, for anti-submarine patrols. Painted on the rear fuselage is Donald Duck, with the words 'We start with the simple knots – Adolph!' (ATP 12209D)

North American Mustang I AG346 at Speke, with the 'temporary' Bellman hangars (Nos 3 and 4) just visible to the right, and two Douglas Bostons and Garston gasworks glimpsed to the left. (ATP 10680D)

North American Mustang II FR901 at Speke in July 1943, with experimental long-range fuel tanks under its wings after fitting by Lockheed. At left, above its wing tip, can be seen one of the small 'blister' hangars built around the airfield during the war. (ATP 12299B)

An informal group of Lockheed workers in front of a Mustang, with the station building in the background. (L. Thompson via Brian Jones)

Two Lockheed mechanics standing on a Lockheed P-38 Lightning of the USAAF, in front of the Ministry of Aircraft Production hangar. The goods sheds in the background, on the other side of Speke Road with the Dunlop advertisement, belong to the LMS Railway. (L. Thompson via Brian Jones)

As the war progressed, Lockheed handled an increasing variety of aircraft types at Speke. The assembly of aircraft for the RAF and Royal Navy was expanded to include similar work for the USAAF; as part of 'reverse Lend-Lease', the British government paid Lockheed to carry out the assembly of these USAAF aircraft. The USAAF types named in the contract included the Fairchild UC-61 (Argus), Cessna UC-78 Bobcat, Lockheed P-38 Lightning, North American AT-6 (Harvard), Noorduyn UC-64 Norseman, North American P-51 Mustang, Piper L-4 Cub and Republic P-47 Thunderbolt, although others were also dealt with, including the Beech C-45 Expediter and the Northrop P-61 Black Widow. Other contracts covered the assembly of aircraft for the British forces, with the named types for the Fleet Air Arm including the Vought Corsair, N.A. Harvard, Grumman Wildcat and Hellcat, Curtiss Helldiver and Beech Traveller. The Lockheed organisation had been called the British Reassembly Division, but on 30 September 1944 it became The Lockheed Aircraft Overseas Corporation.

By the end of 1944, the process of uncrating and assembling thousands of aircraft had begun to go into reverse, with some types beginning to arrive by air from points in Europe to be dismantled for shipment to the USA or elsewhere, and this activity continued well into 1946. The types named in the redeployment contract were the P-38, P-47 and P-51. Not all the records for Speke's individual contribution have survived, but some sample statistics are quoted below, to give an idea of the scale and variety of the activity:

A Grumman Martlet of the Fleet Air Arm, awaiting flight test at Lockheed in 1944. (L. Thompson via Brian Jones)

Output, January 1943 – Speke

For the RAF	North American Mustang fighters	2
	Brewster Bermuda target tugs	32
	Lockheed Ventura medium bombers	2
	Lockheed Hudson VI maritime recce	21
	Lockheed Hudson III maritime recce	1
For the Fleet Air Arm	Grumman Wildcat IV carrier fighters	30
For the USAAF	Lockheed P-38 Lightning fighters	61
	Republic P-47 Thunderbolt fighters	68
	Total of all aircraft	217

Output, October 1943 – Speke

For the RAF	North American Mustang fighters	34
	Brewster Bermuda target tugs	1
	Lockheed Hudson VI maritime recce	1
	Lockheed Hudson III maritime recce	5
	Noorduyn Harvard advanced trainers	56
	Stinson Reliant trainers (RAF and FAA)	38
For the Fleet Air Arm	Grumman Wildcat carrier fighters	4
	Grumman Hellcat carrier fighters	18
	Chance Vought Corsair carrier fighters	2
	Grumman Avenger torpedo bombers	9
For the USAAF	Lockheed P-38 Lightning fighters	21
	Republic P-47 Thunderbolt fighters	27
	North American P-51B Mustang fighters	53
	Cessna UC-78 communications aircraft	5
	Fairchild UC-61 communications aircraft	3
	Piper L-4 Cub liaison aircraft	11
	Total of all aircraft	288

At various times, Lockheed's No.1 Aircraft Assembly Unit at Speke was supported by various other organisations, including BOAC engineers in 1940, by personnel seconded from the Rootes factory, and by both USAAF and RAF personnel. The RAF unit was the Special Servicing Party, American Aircraft (SSPAA), which during 1944 was the largest RAF unit at Speke (approximately 300 officers and men, located in No.2 Hangar). The assembly of short-range aircraft for the Royal Navy and RAF had carried on until late in 1945, and other work had included the conversion of seventy-six Consolidated B-24 Liberator bombers into interim transport aircraft for RAF Transport Command squadrons. Lockheed continued to have a presence at Speke well into 1946 (working now for the USAAF), by which time the emphasis was on returning USAAF short-range aircraft to the USA by sea, after Lockheed had prepared them for shipment.

A Lockheed engineer relaxing in the cowling of a Thunderbolt in 1944. (L. Thompson via Brian Jones)

A snow-covered Thunderbolt with three Lockheed men in front of the Bellman hangar built behind No.1 Hangar. The Banks Road houses are behind. (L. Thompson via Brian Jones)

A view taken from the roof of No.1 Hangar, showing rows of Republic P-47 Thunderbolts in the snow awaiting delivery to the USAAF (probably 9th AAF). (L. Thompson via Brian Jones)

Grumman Wildcat V carrier-borne fighter JV337 for the Fleet Air Arm at Speke, after assembly by Lockheed. (ATP 12261D)

Fairchild UC-61 Forwarder 314468 of the USAAF 8th AAF after assembly at Speke. In RAF service, this type was called the Argus. (RAF Museum P5489)

Lockheed Lightning I AF106 of the RAF at Speke in 1942 – one of only three that came to the UK for RAF evaluation. Several Hurricanes are visible in the background. (Military Aircraft Photographs)

Opposite below: Grumman Wildcats for the Fleet Air Arm being towed from the docks to Speke in June 1944. These aircraft have no protective 'cosmoline' covering, as seen on the Mustangs and Thunderbolts, so have probably arrived on board an aircraft carrier. (Phil Butler collection)

Beech Expediter 335624 of the US 8th AAF in May 1944 after reassembly by the Lockheed unit. (ATP 12852D)

Requisition and Runways

With the threatened outbreak of the Second World War, airline services abruptly ceased, and the airport was taken over for government use. The airport was requisitioned by the Air Ministry from Liverpool Corporation on 31 August 1939, and although in the early days the City Engineer's Department assisted the Air Ministry in various ways, all work on the land and buildings was soon taken over by the Air Ministry Works Department, or civilian contractors chosen by the Air Ministry. The last significant item of work shown in the city council records is the approval of the laying down of a compass base in connection with the Lockheed unit on 29 September 1939 – this could still be seen for many years after the war, the later western apron incorporating its circular structure.

Although RAF Station Speke had by this time been formed under RAF Fighter Command, Speke remained a state airport under the control of the Air Ministry's Director-General of Civil Aviation (DGCA). For the duration of the war, responsibilities were shared between Fighter Command and the DGCA, or shuttled back and forth between the two, with the Ministry of Aircraft Production (which had responsibility for the Lockheed and Rootes operations) occasionally being involved. Thus for most of the war the air traffic control staff were civilian employees of the Air Ministry, some of them having been Liverpool Corporation employees before the outbreak of war. Mr Jack Chadwick of the City Engineer's Department, who had been a member of the airport manager's staff before the war, was seconded to the DGCA, and indeed remained on the Liverpool Corporation payroll at the airport until after it was returned to the corporation in 1961. Ironically, the DGCA civilian controllers were withdrawn only on 12 April 1943; by September of that year the two largest remaining RAF units had been disbanded, leaving only a small communications flight in residence, and on 10 July 1944 RAF Speke itself was disbanded and the airport was handed back to the DGCA.

As for buildings, aprons and runways, almost all the buildings on the north airfield were complete by the end of 1939, with the exception of some of the 'temporary' steel-clad hangars (described under the Lockheed section above). A very narrow concrete apron had been built in 1939 on the airside of the new terminal building, not because the aircraft then in use required anything stronger than a grass surface, but merely to prevent wear and tear causing ruts in the grass during wet weather. Small aprons had also been built outside the main hangars, and at the point where Rootes' Blenheims taxied onto the airfield from the factory.

Only in mid-1941 was a contract agreed with Costains to build a complete hard perimeter track around the airfield boundary. The Costain work included the construction of twelve Blenheim-type concrete dispersal pens on the Speke Hall side of the airfield, some of which were visible until recent times, although the concrete blast-walls surrounding them have long since gone. Various dispersed flight offices and other small buildings were built as part of the Costain contract to serve the aircraft pens; all of these have since been demolished. The Costain drawings show the lines of three proposed hard runways, none of which were constructed. Although the original grass airfield had no marked runways, by 1939 five grass runways had been defined, as below:

Runway No.1	02/20	3,000ft x 600ft
Runway No.2	07/25	4,620ft x 600ft
Runway No.3	11/29	3,240ft x 600ft
Runway No.4	16/34	3,400ft x 600ft
Runway No.5	08/26	5,070ft x 1,200ft

Of these, Runway No.5 was that aligned with the radio approach beacon, and because of this it was later retained in tarmac and concrete form. When it became known that Halifax four-engined heavy bombers were to be built by Rootes, hard runways became absolutely essential, although the first Halifax was to fly on 15 March 1942, rather before A. Monk & Co. Ltd of Warrington started laying the runways on 23 July. The new runways were:

Runway 08/26	5,127ft x 150ft
Runway 04/22	4,187ft x 150ft
Runway 17/35	3,192ft x 150ft

The large western apron, which stretched from No.1 Hangar to the line of Runway 17/35, is believed to have been concreted at the same time as the runways were built.

Royal Air Force Station Speke

The RAF station was centred on the original Auxiliary Air Force camp to the north of the Chapel House Farm buildings. Shortly before the war, this area had been expanded with the erection of more barrack huts and two Bellman hangars to replace the earlier small canvas-covered Bessoneau type. These developments had been intended as a temporary measure pending the construction of a permanent Auxiliary Air Force station on the Speke Hall side of the airfield. The proposed layout would have extended beyond the airfield boundary towards Stockton's Wood, the necessary land having been leased to the Air Ministry before the war started. In the event, only one building of the layout was constructed – the gun butts which still stand on the east side of the north airfield. Other airfield developments for the Air Ministry were also under consideration in the months immediately before the war. After the failure of earlier efforts to attract an RAFVR elementary flying training school to Liverpool, approval had been gained during 1939 for one to be established, and it was in the process of being formed during August of that year. To support this school, the Lamella hangar (most familiarly known as No.2) to the east of the station building had been built at Air Ministry expense, and the school administration facilities and classrooms were being prepared, initially taking over the first floor of the station building. Further land on the east side of the airfield (including the triangle of open land which still exists to the east of the former Rootes factory site) was to be leased for the construction of other RAFVR facilities. The formation of the unit (No.55 Elementary Flying Training School) was cancelled with the mobilisation of the RAF in the days immediately before war was declared.

The personnel of RAF Speke came under No.12 Group, Fighter Command, since their original parent unit (No.611 Squadron) was part of that group. For some weeks after the outbreak of war, Bomber Command Hampden Squadrons spent their days at Speke in case of Luftwaffe attacks on their normal bases in Lincolnshire. This arrangement for dispersal had been planned before the war, and involved several Auxiliary Air Force airfields on the west side of the Pennines. When the dispersal arrangement was found to be unnecessary it ceased, and the Speke personnel found themselves supporting flying by No.5 Service Flying Training School (SFTS) at Sealand, where the circuit had become overloaded with the greater demands of the war, and therefore dispersed some of its operations to Speke and elsewhere.

Finally, on 18 April 1940, the first operational squadron arrived which was to use Speke as its base. This was No.236 Squadron, equipped with Bristol Blenheim IF fighters. The IF was a modified Blenheim I bomber equipped with a gun pack under the fuselage, which was used by Coastal Command, and (when also equipped with radar) as a night fighter. While at Speke, No.236 spent its time training in the day- fighter role. The first squadron aircraft arrived from North Coates on 23 April, but the unit only stayed at Speke until 25 May, when it moved to Filton, near Bristol. At the time the squadron left Speke, it had a strength of seventeen Blenheim IFs. On 16 June 1940, No.13 (Army Co-operation) Squadron arrived, flying across the river from its former base at Hooton Park. No.13 had recently been evacuated from France and was equipped with the Westland Lysander high-wing monoplane. It had been intended that Speke would be transferred to Army Co-operation Command, but this move was cancelled, and after four weeks of uneventful anti-invasion patrols of the coastline from the Solway Firth to south Wales, No.13 Squadron returned to its former base at Hooton Park on 13 July.

On 10 July, No.8 Radio Maintenance Unit had arrived. After a very short period at Speke, this unit set up its headquarters in a large house in Ullet Road, later moving to High Lee, Beaconsfield Road, Woolton (which became Royal Air Force, Woolton). The unit title was a deliberately misleading one, for the unit was actually responsible for building, commissioning and running all the secret defence radar stations in the north-west of England, north Wales, the Isle of Man and Northern Ireland. For this purpose, it operated a Calibration Flight, which continued to be based at Speke for the next three years (although the name of the parent unit at Woolton changed, at first to No.8 Radio Servicing Section, and then to No.77 (Signals) Wing). The flight was equipped with ex-civilian Hornet Moths, which were able to land in small fields adjacent to the actual radar sites on their communications tasks, and larger aircraft (mainly Blenheims) which carried out the actual calibration flying. The first Hornet Moth had been allotted by the time the flight arrived at Speke, and the first Blenheim I arrived on 30 September 1940. In November 1942 the flight was enlarged when

Members of No.77 (Signals) Wing Calibration Flight alongside their 'blister' hangar in 1943. Most of them would be local people with 'compassionate' postings to be based near their homes. (J. Mulheirn)

it absorbed the similar flights of the adjacent No.73 and No.79 Wings. At the time of its disbandment on 18 June 1943, the Calibration Flight had four Hornet Moths, one Oxford and five Blenheim IVs.

The Fighter Squadrons

On 12 September 1940, 141 Polish airmen arrived at Speke to form No.308 (Polish) Squadron of the Royal Air Force. This unit departed for Baginton near Coventry on 25 September, without receiving any aircraft. In the meantime, No.9 Group of Fighter Command had been formed at Barton Hall, north of Preston, to take over the air defence of north-west England, north Wales and the Isle of Man from No.12 Group, which had too large an area to cover. Speke immediately became a sector station of the new group, with its own sector control room and planned permanent fighter squadron. The formation of No.9 Group was a timely one – on the day of its formation four German bombs were dropped on the airport, and other attacks soon followed. The first operational squadron to man the Speke Sector arrived on 26 September, when No.312 (Czech) Squadron flew in from Duxford with their Hawker Hurricane Is. On 8 October 1940, Yellow Section of No.312 Squadron was scrambled when a Junkers Ju 88 was spotted approaching the airport. Three Hurricanes gave chase and the enemy aircraft was shot down near Bromborough, the kill being jointly credited to Flight Lieutenant D.E. Gillam (the RAF liaison officer with the unit), Pilot Officer A. Vasatko and Sergeant J. Stehlik. This was the

A formation of three Hurricanes of No.312 Squadron fly (very) low over another example of the unit on the ground at Speke in 1941. Note the squadron code letters DU on the nearest aircraft. (Phil Butler collection)

only Luftwaffe aircraft shot down to be solely credited to Speke-based fighters, and created something of a record in that the whole combat from take-off to landing of the Hurricanes took only eleven minutes. The victim was a Junkers Ju 88A-1 of 2./Kampfgruppe 806, coded M7+DK, based at Nantes in northern France.

Later experiences of No.312 Squadron were less fortunate. Two days after the combat, Sergeant Pilot Hanzlicek was killed when his Hurricane crashed in the River Mersey, while on 13 October 312 Squadron attacked a formation of No.29 Squadron Blenheims over Liverpool Bay, shooting down one aircraft and damaging another. This mishap arose from the similarity of the British Blenheim to the German Ju 88, which led to all too numerous tragedies of mistaken identity during the early war years. On 15 October, No.312 Squadron lost three aircraft when the pilots became lost, ran out of fuel and had to bale out. After this, the squadron settled down to a routine of training flights and defensive patrols until the unit departed to RAF Valley on 3 March 1941. On 22 December 1940, No.229 Squadron arrived to bring Speke up to a two-squadron station. This squadron also flew Hurricane Is and arrived from RAF Wittering. It joined in the routine established by No.312, until the unit left for the Middle East on 19 May 1941, the pilots having embarked on the aircraft carrier HMS *Furious* some days earlier. Meanwhile, on 13 March 1941, No.312 Squadron had been replaced by No.315 (Polish) Squadron, which arrived from Acklington, again with Hawker Hurricanes. This squadron moved to Northolt on 10 July, where it was to be re-equipped with Spitfires, after a relatively uneventful time at Speke.

With the departure of No.229 Squadron, Speke became a single-squadron station once again. This allowed space for the formation of other units, and on 25 May

1941 two second-line units formed. Firstly, Station Flight Speke was formed and was allotted a Miles Magister (for communications duties) and two Hawker Hurricanes. The Hurricanes were intended to provide local air defence for the Rootes factory on occasions when the based fighter squadron was on patrol away from the airfield. The second unit was No.9 Group Anti-Aircraft Co-operation Flight, whose task was to provide practice targets for AA batteries within the No.9 Group area. This unit was equipped with Westland Lysanders and Bristol Blenheims, and stayed until moving to RAF Wrexham (Borras) in August 1941. Other second-line units had appeared earlier in the year – on 4 January 1941 Liverpool University Air Squadron had been formed, although it was not until 28 April that the squadron's one Tiger Moth was delivered to Speke. On the same day an impressed civilian Gipsy Moth was also allotted, but on arrival it was taken by road to the unit's headquarters in Liverpool and used for ground instruction purposes. On 31 March a detachment of No.116 Squadron equipped with Lysanders had arrived, to provide targets for calibrating AA guns; this detachment departed to Hucknall at the end of April, but returned (from Hooton Park) on 11 June 1942, before finally departing to Woodvale on 15 November 1942.

Coinciding with the departure of No.315 Squadron to Northolt on 10 July 1941, No.303 (Polish) Squadron arrived from that base, bringing in its Spitfire IIs. No.303 returned to Northolt on 7 October, changing places with No.306 (Polish) Squadron, which became the last fighter squadron to serve the Speke Sector. No.306 left for Church Stanton on 11 December 1941; on that date RAF Woodvale opened, and took over as the fighter airfield for the defence of Merseyside, although No.9 Group's presence at Speke continued with the MSFU, below.

A staged photograph showing pilots of No.312 Squadron running to their aircraft at Speke in 1940. The pilot in the dark flying suit is F/L D.E. Gillam, DSO, DFC, AFC. The other pilots are F/L Jaske and Sergeant Pilots Truhlar, Slouf, Stehlik and Janeba. (Phil Butler collection, via Alan Davie)

This Junkers Ju 88A shot down at Bromborough by No.312 Squadron on 8 October 1940. The Junkers was coded 'M7+DK' and belonged to 2/KGr.806, a Luftwaffe naval reconnaissance and co-operation unit. (Phil Butler collection)

Merchant Ship Fighter Unit

Possibly the most interesting and important RAF unit to be based at Speke was the Merchant Ship Fighter Unit (MSFU), formed on 5 May 1941. The role of this unit was to provide aircraft and crews to serve on board merchant ships sailing on convoy escort duties. The aircraft was the Sea Hurricane, which was to be mounted on board suitably equipped catapult aircraft merchant ships (or 'CAM-ships'). The crew consisted of a fighter pilot, a fighter direction officer (usually a naval officer), and airframe and engine fitters to carry out routine maintenance. The fighter pilots were volunteers drawn from Fighter Command squadrons, and the unit came under No.9 Group in the same way as the Speke-based fighter squadrons. The unit was formed because at the time there were insufficient aircraft carriers to provide convoy escorts. The fighter's role was primarily a deterrent one. If launched to defend the convoy, usually against Luftwaffe Focke-Wulf Condor long-range reconnaissance aircraft, the Hurricane was to fly to the nearest land if within range. If this was not possible (as was usually the case) the pilot was to bale out near the convoy in the hope of being picked up. The catapult used for pilot training at Speke was installed on a concrete base to the south of No.2 Hangar (which, much later, became a helicopter landing pad). The catapult itself had previously been used for experimental purposes at

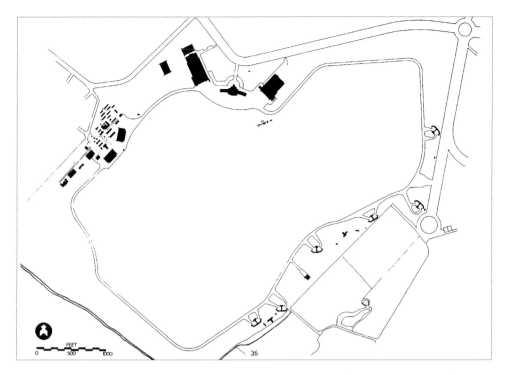

A map of the airfield layout in 1941. The item within the perimeter track near No.2 Hangar is the catapult for the Merchant Ship Fighter Unit.

RAE Farnborough, and arrived at Speke on 8 May 1941, making its first launch on 6 July 1941 with Hurricane V7253. The unit establishment was large, comprising fifty operational Hurricane Is. In practice Sea Hurricanes were used because they were already equipped for catapulting. The unit also held a Tiger Moth for communications duties, and five Hurricanes plus one reserve for catapult training and general continuation training of pilots temporarily on shore. The catapult training section of MSFU was briefly called the Catapult Training and Development Establishment, but was soon absorbed into the MSFU itself.

The CAM-ships were mainly employed on Atlantic convoy work, and although many sailed from the Mersey (meaning that the aircraft were loaded by crane at Birkenhead, Liverpool or Ellesmere Port), Glasgow was also frequently used, with Belfast, Barry and Avonmouth used to a lesser extent. In these cases, the Hurricanes were flown to Abbotsinch, Sydenham, St Athan, or Filton before being transported by road to the docks. At first, on the completion of a voyage, the reverse crane and road transport process was used, but later the aircraft were catapulted off when within range of a suitable airfield and flown back to Speke where they were inspected and then usually flown away for major maintenance after suffering the rigours of a further sea voyage. Similar arrangements were made at RCAF Dartmouth in Nova Scotia, which was close to the main assembly and dispersal point for Atlantic convoys. Later,

Sea Hurricane IA Z4935 of the Merchant Ship Fighter Unit being mounted on the catapult by a crane. The long items leaning against the back of the catapult are the rockets used to propel the launching trolley. The MSFU had a large number of aircraft, so it used code letters LU- and NJ- as well the KE- marking shown on this Hurricane. (IWM CH15390)

CAM-ships were used on convoys to Gibraltar and north Russia and in these cases reserve aircraft and maintenance parties were located at North Front, Gibraltar, and Keg Ostrov, Archangel. From October 1942, with the increasing availability of escort carriers built primarily for convoy escort duties, the need for CAM-ships decreased, and the unit establishment was reduced to an initial equipment of ten Sea Hurricane IAs, nine Hurricane IAs and one Master II.

Although the long-term existence of the unit was in doubt, extensive trials took place with the prototype Seafire L.IIC from August 1942, including twenty-five launches from the catapult at Speke, and at least one launch from the CAM-ship MV *Daghestan* and it was concluded that the Seafire was more suitable for catapult launching than the Sea Hurricane. Although some Spitfires were received for training, when re-equipment came it was with the Sea Hurricane IC, and in January 1943 ten of the existing Sea Hurricane IAs were despatched to General Aircraft Ltd at Hanworth to have Mk.IIC-type wings fitted to bring them up to the new standard (Mk.IIC wings each had two 20mm cannon fitted in place of four .303in machine guns). The Mk.IC versions were issued to the MSFU during May 1943, but little operational use was made of them, and the unit disbanded on 7 September 1943.

The MSFU used at least 130 different Hurricanes during its life, and we have included the history of one of these to give some idea of the work of the unit. Hurricane V7653 was a presentation aircraft named *Jagirdars II*, after a group in India which had subscribed for the purchase of a Hurricane. It was built by Hawker against a contract for 496 aircraft placed towards the end of 1939. It was delivered to No.19 MU St Athan on 27 October 1940. After RAF service with Nos 145, 32 and 306 Squadrons, it was delivered to General Aircraft Ltd at Hanworth for conversion to Sea Hurricane standard on 14 June 1941 and was delivered to the MSFU at Speke on 13 July. On 24 July it flew to Abbotsinch near Glasgow and on 18 August was loaded on board the CAM-ship SS *Helencrest*. The ship sailed from Gourock to Halifax, Nova Scotia, on 25 August with V7653 and MSFU crew No.28. V7653 was offloaded to RCAF Dartmouth for servicing, later being reloaded on the same ship, as was the usual practice. The *Helencrest* arrived back at Avonmouth on 21 October 1941, V7653 having been catapult-launched in the Bristol Channel on the previous day and flown to Speke. V7653 then flew on to No.13 MU Henlow for major inspection and by 1 November was at No.29 MU High Ercall in storage, being temporarily surplus to MSFU requirements. On 3 July 1942, V7653 flew back to Speke and on 15 August was allocated to the CAM-ship *Empire Morn*, which was about to sail to north Russia with convoy PQ.18. On 18 September the aircraft was launched at position 68 degrees

The same Sea Hurricane being launched. The 'catapult' was just a trolley running on rails, the motive power being the six cordite rockets attached to the trolley. The aircraft was launched from a ship in the same manner. The naval Sea Hurricane was used because it was already equipped for catapulting. (IWM CH15395)

Another MSFU Sea Hurricane, V6756 NJ-L, mounted on the catapult of the CAM-ship *Empire Tide*. (IWM A9422)

30 minutes north, 42 degrees 30 minutes east, and fought an inconclusive battle with a Heinkel He 111 which was attacking the convoy. Since the convoy was by that time close to land, V7653 was able to land at Keg Ostrov aerodrome, Archangel. By 13 December, V7653 was back in England and was allocated to David Rosenfield Ltd at Barton for a major inspection. It did not return to the MSFU.

Two other units flew from Speke. First was No.15 Group Communications Flight, which arrived from Hooton Park on 15 December 1942. No.15 Group belonged to Coastal Command and was primarily concerned with anti-submarine warfare in the western approaches to the UK. The group HQ was in Liverpool, where it worked closely with the Admiralty HQ Western Approaches in Derby House. The flight was quite a small unit, its strength in January 1944 being only fifteen personnel, and it usually had no more than three or four aircraft, mainly twin-engined communications types such as the Percival Q-6, Airspeed Oxford or DH Dominie. However, by 1944 it was the only RAF flying unit remaining at Speke, and it remained almost until the end of the war, being disbanded in August 1945. The final unit to be mentioned is No.186 Elementary Gliding School – not strictly an RAF unit – which was formed in June 1944 to provide gliding training for local Air Training Corps cadets. The school had various elementary gliders such as Slingsby Kirby Cadets, and flew from Speke until early 1947 when it moved to Hooton Park. In later years this school moved to Woodvale and then Hawarden. While at Hawarden in 1955 it was renumbered No.631 Gliding School, and later moved to RAF Sealand, where it still exists today.

Fleet Air Arm

The Fleet Air Arm arrived at Speke on 27 March 1941 in the form of No.776 Squadron. This was a second-line unit performing fleet requirements duties, such as towing gunnery targets, radar calibration, and communications flying for the local naval headquarters. The first aircraft to arrive were Blackburn Roc torpedo bombers modified as target tugs, but during its life at Speke the squadron operated an immense variety of aircraft. One duty was to provide a communications aircraft for the Commander-in-Chief, Western Approaches, whose HQ was in Derby House in Liverpool, and his first aircraft arrived on 24 June 1941. No.776 always provided the mainstay of the Fleet Air Arm presence at Speke, although many of its operations were in fact performed from Woodvale and other nearby airfields. The unit was based in No.39 Hangar for most of its time at Speke, which did not end until 7 April 1945, when it finally moved to Woodvale. Speke never became a Royal Naval Air Station, the administration of the FAA units being in the hands of a naval air section of RAF Speke. Other FAA squadrons were based at Speke, usually for very short periods while preparing to fly on to Mersey-based escort carriers. Of these units, the longest residence was by No.1832 Squadron, a first-line fighter unit equipped with Grumman Martlets, which arrived on 20 September 1943 and finally departed on 2 February 1944. This squadron had a number of Flights, each allocated to one of the Liverpool-based escort carriers. Full details of the other FAA squadrons associated with Speke are shown in Appendix 3.

Wartime Airline Operations

As recorded earlier, airline services to Dublin, Belfast and the Isle of Man (and elsewhere) ceased at the end of August 1939, but the routes over the Irish Sea were reinstated before the end of 1939 under National Air Communications control, flown by the former airline operators. In May 1940 some changes were made to these operations. From 6 May, West Coast Air Services joined Aer Lingus in the operation of the Liverpool–Dublin route, and on the same day Railway Air Services reopened a daily Glasgow–Belfast–Liverpool service with DH.86s. The Isle of Man Air Services' Liverpool–Isle of Man service had been reduced to two daily, but from 6 May it was restored to four flights daily until 29 September, after which the fourth flight of the day only operated if there was sufficient traffic. In practice all the West Coast, Railway Air Services and Isle of Man Air Service schedules were subject to severe disruption during May and June because the aircraft were required to assist with the evacuation of the RAF from France. From 6 May internal airline operations had been made the responsibility of the Associated Airways Joint Committee, but the AAJC only really became operational from 27 June after the release of the aircraft from evacuation duties. The Associated Airways Joint Committee comprised Railway Air Services, West Coast Air Services, Isle of Man Air Services, Scottish Airways, Great Western & Southern Airlines, Air Commerce and Olley Air Service, and had a total fleet of

The Railway Air Services DH86 G-ACZP. Although the photograph was first published at the time the Liverpool–Croydon service was restarted in 1944, it is believed to have been taken in 1942. Note the wartime camouflage on the aircraft and the red, white and blue lines under the aircraft's registration. The windows are blanked out to prevent the passengers from seeing Mersey shipping and other sensitive sights. (British Rail Publicity Department)

four DH.86s, fourteen Rapides and two Dragons. The AAJC was administered from the Railway Air Services Headquarters in London, but its engineering base was at Speke, employing about seventy-five personnel and using the former Liverpool Aero Club hangar to the west of Chapel House Farm. The engineering base covered major maintenance on aircraft from all the operators who flew services from Land's End to the Scilly Isles and from the Scottish mainland to Orkney, Shetland and the main Hebridean islands, as well as the flights from Liverpool. From 5 August 1940, the Liverpool–Dublin service was transferred to Manchester (Barton) for security reasons (so that passengers travelling from neutral Ireland could not observe Mersey shipping), and remained there until 16 November 1942. The West Coast aircraft operating the service were still based at Speke and positioned to Barton each day. After the relaxation of the security regulations, the Dublin service operated normally from Speke until 14 April 1944 when the service was suspended, again for security reasons, until after the invasion of Europe in June, being started again on 8 September 1944. The aircraft used on the Dublin route were normally DH.86s, although Aer Lingus had sometimes used their Lockheed 14s in 1939–40, and on 7 May 1940 used their new Douglas DC-3 EI-ACA for the first time, this aircraft continuing to be employed when traffic demands were heavy. The AAJC was concerned at its image in using old biplanes in competition with the DC-3 and attempted to obtain a modern DH Flamingo for the route, but to no avail.

Another Railway Air Services DH86, G-AENR, in front of the terminal in 1942. (Phil Butler collection)

It is interesting to note that in 1942 the wartime airline services carried more passengers from Speke than in any pre-war year, even though the capacity offered and the choice of routes was obviously reduced. In fact the Liverpool–Isle of Man service was the most popular of the AAJC network, and in 1941 operated at 87 per cent capacity. The secret was that airline services were beginning to be appreciated and becoming commonplace. The Liverpool–Isle of Man services continued to be run for the duration of the war by Isle of Man Air Services Rapides, usually with three flights each weekday in winter and four in summer. The Liverpool–Belfast–Glasgow service of Railway Air Services had started as a once-daily operation, but as from 1 September 1941 an additional daily DH.86 Liverpool–Belfast flight was introduced (mainly to carry mail), and by 1943 a further additional daily Rapide flight to Belfast was added, bringing the Liverpool–Belfast services to three flights each weekday. Finally, towards the end of the war, the services were expanded by the introduction of a daily extension of one of the Belfast–Liverpool DH.86 flights to London (Croydon) from 13 November 1944, and then the introduction of a daily Glasgow–Liverpool–Croydon Rapide flight from 9 April 1945. (Of the other four AAJC companies, GW&S Airlines flew from Land's End to the Scilly Isles, Scottish Airways flew from Glasgow to the Hebrides, Orkneys and Shetlands, while Olley and Air Commerce flew government charter flights.)

4

Return of Peace

Wartime restrictions prevailed for some time after the end of the war itself, and general civilian flying was not permitted until 1 January 1946, although the Associated Airways Joint Committee internal air routes continued without interruption. Those operating in February 1946 were as follows:

Isle of Man Air Services Ltd	Liverpool–Isle of Man	3 flights each weekday
Railway Air Services Ltd	Liverpool–Belfast	2 flights each weekday
	London–Liverpool–Belfast	3 flights each weekday
	London–Liverpool–Glasgow	1 flight each weekday
West Coast Air Services Ltd	Liverpool–Dublin	2 flights each weekday
Aer Lingus Teoranta	Liverpool–Dublin	2 flights each weekday

All these services were flown by the DH.86s and Rapides that had been in use during the war, although during 1946 Railway Air Services introduced new Avro XIXs, equivalent to the RAF Anson C.19, that were certainly used on some Liverpool services. It was also intended to introduce the Junkers Ju 52/3m, which was available from stocks captured in Germany, and indeed one such aircraft was delivered to the AAJC maintenance base at Speke on 10 January 1946 to be prepared for service.

At this time the internal air services in the UK were in a state of flux because the new Labour government had decreed the formation of the nationalised British European Airways Corporation to take over all domestic and European air routes. The formation of the new airline took a considerable time to arrange and it did not actually operate its own services until early in 1947. In the meantime, the private companies ran their existing routes, and in some cases they continued to do so under charter to the British European Airways Corporation (BEAC or, more usually, BEA) after it became operational, because of its own aircraft and crew shortages.

The former Associated Airways Joint Committee maintenance base at Speke continued to service aircraft for most of the AAJC airlines, and in 1947 it became the base of the English Division of the BEAC, responsible for maintenance of the Rapide, Avro XIX and Dakota fleets.

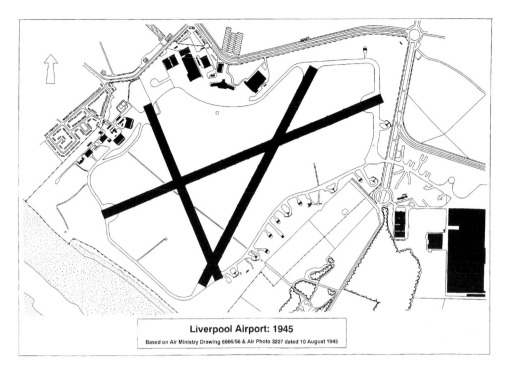

Liverpool Airport: 1945
Based on Air Ministry Drawing 6866/56 & Air Photo 3207 dated 10 August 1945

The airport layout as it was in August 1945, showing what was later called the north airfield, with the adjacent Rootes factory site. Speke Hall lies approximately below the right-hand end of the title box on the drawing. (Drawing by Paul Francis)

The first private airline to cease operations from Speke was West Coast Air Services, which stopped flying on 30 June 1946. This was because of an agreement between the British and Irish governments that allowed Aer Lingus to have a monopoly of all air services between the UK and Ireland for a period of ten years from 1 July 1946. From that date Aer Lingus operated five flights daily from Liverpool to Dublin, using DH.86s EI-ABK and EI-ABT. On 18 November 1946, Railway Air Services introduced Junkers Ju 52/3m Jupiters on their Croydon–Liverpool–Belfast route, these being in British European Airways colours, but flown by Railway Air Services crews. Finally, on 1 February 1947 all Railway Air Services and Isle of Man Air Services routes were taken over by British European Airways, all (with the exception of the Ju 52s on the London–Liverpool–Belfast route) being flown by Avro XIXs and Rapides. By this time Aer Lingus had introduced the Douglas DC-3 (Dakota) on the Dublin service, the DH.86s having been sold at the end of the 1946 summer season.

A panoramic photograph taken on 10 August 1945, showing the airfield, Speke Hall and the Rootes aircraft factory. There are many large crates lying in Speke Hall Avenue and in the Hall grounds, and rows of Mustangs awaiting return to the USA. Larger aircraft include Consolidated Liberator bombers, awaiting conversion to transports by Lockheed. (Phil Butler collection)

No.1 Hangar and the 'temporary' hangars around it on 10 August 1945. Nos 3 and 4 Hangars, nearest to Banks Road, have Mustangs outside. No.5 Hangar is at the back of No.1, and No.6 on the landward side of No.1. The large aircraft are Consolidated Liberators, with a Lockheed Hudson behind the group of three Liberators. The circular area set in the apron is the compass base (used for adjusting the magnetic compasses in aircraft). At the bottom is a small Robin hangar in the Bryant & May sports field, one of several used to disperse aircraft off the main airfield.

Right: Another photograph from 10 August 1945, showing the terminal building and the main No.1 and No.2 Hangars. The large building alongside the entrance road is Lockheed's (later BEA's) canteen.

Below: North American Mustangs of the USAAF at Speke in 1945. The nearest example is an F-6 photo-reconnaissance version formerly of the 69th Tactical Reconnaissance Group (note the camera-port below the star). These aircraft were being prepared for shipment back to the USA. (IWM EA.74243)

Republic P-47 Thunderbolts of the US 9th AAF also awaiting return to the USA in 1945 – although in reality many were probably reduced to scrap metal. (Phil Butler collection)

A busy apron at Speke on 1 April 1946, with many Railway Air Services de Havilland aircraft on view. There are two DH.86s (G-ACVY and G-AENR) and five Rapides (with more out of shot). (Liverpool Record Office)

DH Rapide G-AGSI of Olley Air Service, photographed in 1946, still with the wartime red, white and blue stripes and fin flash. Olley Air Service was one of the Speke-based AAJC companies, operating charter flights, while Gordon Olley was the deputy general manager of the AAJC. (John Stroud)

Government Policy

At the time, government policy affected not only the operations of airlines by in effect placing them under the monopoly direction of British European Airways, but also the airports in general, because it was the policy that all airports used by scheduled air services would be operated by the Ministry of Civil Aviation. In line with this policy, airports requisitioned by the Air Ministry for war purposes remained under requisition, their powers being transferred to the new Ministry of Civil Aviation. In other cases, airports that, for one reason or another, had not been requisitioned were purchased outright by the ministry from their former owners. Speke came into the former category, along with most of the other major pre-war provincial airports such as Glasgow, Bristol and Birmingham. Manchester's Ringway was a significant exception, because Manchester had refused to accept requisitioning in 1939, and had reached an alternative arrangement with the authorities, whereby the City of Manchester retained ownership of its airport while permitting its use for war purposes.

The flaw which became apparent in the official policy was that, although the provincial airports received relatively equal-handed treatment in the provision of new facilities, ministerial bureaucracy ensured that no new facility was provided until the need for it had been demonstrated in triplicate, which had a stifling effect on innovation and development. Equally stifling was the inability of the civil servants charged with day-to-day running of the airports to become involved in attracting new traffic,

Above: A scene in 1947, showing a DH Rapide G-AGUR, Avro XIXs G-AHII and G-AHIE, and Junkers Ju 52/3m G-AHOJ awaiting passengers. (*Liverpool Daily Post*)

Opposite:
Top: DH.86 G-ADYH of Skytravel in front of the station building at Speke in 1946. (P.H. Butler collection)

Middle: Airspeed Consul G-AIOL of Steiners Air Services, named *Liverpool Hawk*, photographed in 1947. Steiners' aircraft were painted silver with red markings. (E.J. Riding, via Peter Green)

Bottom: Avro Lancastrian G-AHBZ *Sky Ambassador* of Skyways Ltd, during the 1948 'milk lift' from Belfast. Note the milk churns and the Bryant & May works in the background. (A.J. Jackson collection)

promoting the use of existing facilities, or publicising anything connected with their airport in anything but the most guarded terms, for fear of being seen to favour one airport, operation or service against another.

Nevertheless, in 1946 the effect that the government policies were to have was not appreciated and lay some time in the future. Liverpool Airport at the time had facilities that compared favourably with any other in the country and in most respects the airport seemed set for further steady development. The maintenance base for the BEA English Division was on a larger scale than the previous AAJC operation, and the airline services already flying continued into 1947. Because of the use of longer-range aircraft, the London–Liverpool–Glasgow service was withdrawn in favour of direct London–Glasgow flights, and the London–Liverpool–Belfast flights were reduced for the same reason.

Although British European Airways had a monopoly on all scheduled air services, private companies were permitted to operate charter flights and tourist services, and privately owned charter companies started up in large numbers such that almost every airfield worth the name had its local operator. Speke was no exception, and in June 1946 Skytravel became the first to establish itself at Liverpool, starting with one Auster Autocrat, but soon adding Proctors, Consuls, Aerovans, DH.86s and further Austers. Skytravel's operations were divided between Liverpool and Blackpool Airports and included local pleasure flying at both airports as well as frequent charter flights to the Isle of Man and other destinations. Skytravel was forced into liquidation in August 1947, the fleet being repossessed by Bowmakers, the finance company that had funded the lease-purchase of their aircraft.

A second charter operator was Steiner's Air and Travel Services, started by D.L. Steiner, a Belgian national who owned a car sales business in Dovedale Road, Liverpool. This firm started in October 1946 with a Proctor 5 and an ex-Aer Lingus DH.86, soon adding Rapides, Ansons and Consuls. These too were employed on pleasure flying and charter operations, including frequent flights to the Isle of Man. Another aspect of the operation was the flying of newspapers (such as the *Irish Times*) from Dublin to Liverpool for distribution in England. This contract showed another weakness in the operation of the BEA monopoly – Steiner was threatened with prosecution for running a scheduled service because of the regular pattern of their Anson and Rapide flights from Dublin to Liverpool. No doubt because of this hostile environment, Mr Steiner closed down his air charter operation towards the end of 1947, returning to his motor business, although the airline name lived on as a travel agency.

Other charter flights made a noticeable impact on the airport's fortunes in 1947, with the introduction of the milk lift in September and October, arising from severe milk shortages in England. To counter the shortage a major air freight operation was mounted to fly milk in churns from Northern Ireland to Speke, the flights being made from Belfast (Nutts Corner) by four Avro Lancastrians of Skyways Ltd.

By 1948, some changes began to appear in the commercial aviation scene. Although an attempt by Aer Lingus to compete directly with British European Airways by operating a Dublin–Belfast–Liverpool service with Vikings (starting on 6 October 1947) came to nothing, it came to be realised that the British European Airways monopoly of all internal and continental scheduled services was unrealistic.

1 A poster advertising the air display for the official opening of Liverpool Airport by the Secretary of State for Air on Saturday 1 July 1933. (Phil Dale)

2 Douglas DC-3 Pionair-class G-AHCV of British European Airways, at Speke on 4 April 1960, shortly before the type was withdrawn from service. (Phil Dale)

3 Starways Douglas DC-4 G-APYK outside Starways' new hangar on the Speke Road frontage, east of the terminal area, in 1960. This was the third of Starways' Skymasters to be delivered, all of them second-hand examples from airlines in the USA, the type being in service from 1957 to 1963. (Peter Whalley)

4 British Eagle Bristol Britannia G-AOVT Enterprise at Speke on New Year's Day 1964. This is the aircraft that flew the first London–Liverpool service after the route was taken over from Starways. British Eagle Britannias were regular visitors until the airline's demise in November 1968. (Phil Dale)

5 Harry Paterson's Fox Moth G-AOJH waiting for pleasure-flight customers in the 1960s. This Fox Moth was a post-war Canadian-built example, based at Liverpool for several years. (Don Stephens)

6 Cambrian Viscount 701 G-AMON at Speke, October 1965. Cambrian acquired a number of Viscount 701s from BEA early in 1963 and introduced them on the Irish Sea routes in place of BEA. Later they were used on other internal and inclusive tour services from Liverpool. (Don Stephens)

7 British Eagle BAC 1-11 G-ATTP Swift on the day of the opening of the new runway, 7 May 1966. Thereafter, British Eagle used their 1-11 fleet on many services from Liverpool. (Ken Fielding)

8 British Airways Viscount 802 G-AOJF at Speke in March 1977. This was a familiar sight on the apron for many years, until replaced by aircraft of British Midland in 1982. (Phil Butler)

9 Bond Helicopters Aérospatiale Dauphin 2 G-BLEY at Liverpool Airport in May 1995. Bond Helicopters maintained an essential service to oil and gas rigs in the Irish Sea from 1994 to 1998. (Gerry Manning)

10 Emerald Airways HS.748 G-OJEM at Speke in July 1997. Emerald was a major freight and mail carrier after it arrived in 1993, also for some time flying passenger services to the Isle of Man with its HS.748s. (Gerry Manning)

11 *Above:* EasyJet Boeing 737 G-EZYI photographed from the new terminal building at Liverpool in July 2003, where easyJet operated ten Liverpool routes. The 737 has been largely replaced by Airbus A319s. (Phil Butler)

14 *Opposite below:* Ryanair Boeing 737 EI-CON at Liverpool in July 2003. This was a 'Classic' 200-series 737, no replaceed by the 'New-Generation' 800 series. (Phil Butler)

12 Manx Airlines BAe ATP G-PEEL at Liverpool Airport in March 1991. The BAe ATP (Advanced Turbo Prop), developed from the earlier HS.748, was the mainstay of Manx Airlines (and BA CitiExpress) Irish Sea operations from Liverpool. (Gerry Manning)

13 British Airways Concorde G-BOAA during one of its 'Grand National Day' visits to Liverpool Airport on 10 April 1999. Concorde made a total of eighty-eight flights to and from Liverpool before it was retired in 2003. (Phil Butler)

16 Ryanair Boeing 737-800 EI-DCS during its landing approach to Runway 27 at Liverpool John Lennon Airport on 3 May 2005. (Phil Butler)

17 An easyJet Airbus A319-111, G-EZNM, making an approach to Runway 27. (Phil Butler)

15 *Opposite:* The original control tower, centre-piece of the 1938 Station Building, following its restoration as the Liverpool Marriott South Hotel. (Phil Butler)

18 An Airbus A320 of the Hungarian low-cost airline Wizzair at Liverpool John Lennon in September 2007. (Adrian Thompson)

19 The British airline FlyBe (otherwise Jersey European Airways) flew a number of services from John Lennon during 2005–08, mainly using the very economical twin prop-jet de Havilland DHC-8-400 (the 'Dash 8'). (Phil Butler)

20 The Liverpool-based airline Emerald Airways flew many freight and mail services from Liverpool in the 1993–2006 period. This photograph shows G-JEMC, one of the British Aerospace Advanced Turboprops (ATPs) used on its passenger services to the Isle of Man. (Phil Butler)

21 Aer Lingus made a welcome return to Liverpool between 2004 and 2006 and this photograph shows one of their Airbus A320s, EI-CVB, landing at Liverpool. (Phil Butler)

22 One of the short-lived passenger operations that took place during 2005 was the unsuccessful airline Air Wales, one of whose ATR-42 turboprops, G-TAWE, is seen here. The airline flew from Cardiff to Newcastle and back, via Liverpool, but later abandoned all its services. The ATR-42 was also used by Aer Arran, whose aircraft still fly on the EuroManx Isle of Man route. (Phil Butler)

23 The three Cessna Citation executive jets of the Liverpool-based company AD Aviation, in front of the Ravenair hangar on the 'General Aviation' parking area, close to the eastern end of the airport. (Adrian Thompson)

24 The main scheduled freight service from Liverpool is now the one flown by TNT to Liege in Belgium, where the company has its main European 'hub'. The company uses a variety of aircraft of its own, but also the 'classic' Lockheed Electra turboprop chartered from Atlantic Airlines of Coventry. This example is G-LOFE. (Dave Graham)

25 Fokker F-50 OO-VLY of the Belgian airline VLM, which operated the service from Liverpool to London City Airport for a number of years. (Dave Graham)

26 Two Boeing 757 airliners of Flyglobespan at Liverpool John Lennon Airport. Flyglobespan is an airline based in Scotland, which started services to New York and Toronto from Liverpool in 2007. (Adrian Thompson)

27 The Isle of Man based operator EuroManx flies from Liverpool to Ronaldsway Airport in the island five times per day. This shot shows OE-HBC, one of the airline's DHC-8s (a smaller version than the FlyBe type shown in an earlier photograph). (Adrian Thompson)

29 *Opposite below:* An exercise by Liverpool Airport fire-fighters, using the training rig which has been built at the airport. This is also available for training crews from other airports. (Liverpool John Lennon Airport)

28 One of the fire tender used by the airport's own fire service. Fortunately, although it has been called upon to attend to minor incidents, they have never had to attend any major accidents, but it is good to know that they are there. (Graham Ward)

30 A view of the landside of the terminal building at John Lennon Airport. (Liverpool John Lennon Airport)

31 One of the 'Cobus' transfer buses used by John Lennon Airport to take passengers between the terminal building and aircraft parked on remote stands – quite different vehicles from the 1935 coach shown earlier in the book. (Adrian Thompson)

The tourist services run by charter operators in 1946–47 (many of which were barely distinguishable from scheduled operations which were legally forbidden) had shown a strong public demand for seasonal air services, which BEA clearly did not have the resources to operate. It was therefore agreed that in future the privately owned charter companies might run scheduled routes, provided that they negotiated an associate agreement with BEA which safeguarded the state airline's interests. Thus, the agreements strictly laid down operating frequencies, capacities and periods of operation, which rarely (if ever) exceeded one year. The first service of this nature known to have operated to Speke was by Patrick Duval Aviation, with a daily Birmingham–Liverpool operation in 1949.

Thus, the agreements strictly laid down operating frequencies, capacities and periods of operation, which rarely (if ever) exceeded one year. The first service of this nature known to have operated to Speke was by Patrick Duval Aviation, with a daily Birmingham–Liverpool operation in 1949.

Pure 'charter flights' were still unrestricted. The highlight of 1948 was the running of another milk lift, which operated from 20 August on a much larger scale than the previous year. As before, the charterer was the Milk Marketing Board. The operation involved flying 30,000 gallons of milk per day from Belfast (Nutts Corner) to Speke (with additional quantities being flown from Belfast to Squires Gate). The milk was carried in ten-gallon churns, and since a DC-3 carried 70 churns and a Halifax transported 110, some twenty-five to thirty flights per day were required. The operation involved the following airlines and aircraft:

Scottish Airlines	2 Dakota, 2 Liberator
Bond Air Services	1 Halifax
British American Air Services	2 Halifax
Ciro's Aviation	1 Dakota
World Air Freight	1 Halifax
Air Transport (Charter)	2 Dakota
Lancashire Aircraft Corp	2 Halifax

The intensity of the operation resulted in a number of accidents, but the only one directly involving Liverpool was a spectacular belly landing by a Scottish Airlines Liberator on 13 October 1948, which ended up a few feet from the terminal building. The aircraft was written off, although crew and churns escaped without injury. The 'milk lift' ended on 28 October 1948.

The extent of charter flights by smaller operators is illustrated by the arrivals on the day of the Grand National on 20 March 1948. This is always an Irish-dominated occasion, and the largest aircraft bringing racegoers was the Aer Lingus Lockheed L.749 Constellation EI-ADE. However, the majority of flights were by small aircraft with three to eight passenger seats, and the event drew eight Auster Autocrats, two Fairchild Argus, four Avro Ansons, twenty-three Airspeed Consuls, a Cessna Airmaster, Miles Magister, DH Hornet Moth, Douglas Dakota, Bristol 170, Miles Falcon, five DH Doves, a Vickers Viking, two Miles Messengers, a Percival Q.6, eight Miles Gemini, a

The terminal building in 1948, with a British European Airways Dakota (G-AJIC) disembarking passengers. (BEA)

DH Rapide G-AGLR of British European Airways at Speke in 1948. (Phil Butler collection)

Avro XIX G-AHID of British European Airways in 1948. (Phil Butler collection)

Douglas Dakota G-AGIU of British European Airways, with Avro XIX G-AHIG behind, in front of No.1 Hangar, in 1948. (Phil Butler collection)

Halifax, Piper Cub, twelve Percival Proctors and twenty-seven DH Rapides (a total of 102 aircraft). This record number for a single event has never been beaten!

BEA itself was having problems. By the end of 1947, the Avro XIX and Junkers Ju 52 fleets had been withdrawn and the Rapide fleet severely cut back in order to standardise on the Dakota as far as possible, and the use of the larger aircraft meant the rationalisation or abandonment of many peripheral routes. Due to lack of passenger demand, the winter 1947–48 timetables saw the combination of the Liverpool–London and Manchester–London services as a once-daily Liverpool–Manchester–London Dakota, and even this was withdrawn entirely in April 1948. The rationalisation of the aircraft fleets led in turn to a reduced maintenance workload, hence causing a rationalisation of this area also. During 1948 the English and Scottish Divisions of BEA were amalgamated as the British Division, and it was announced that the division would have only one engineering base, at Glasgow (Renfrew). Despite protests by MPs and local authorities, the Speke base was duly shut down between January and March 1949.

Despite the problems described above, the Ministry of Civil Aviation still considered Liverpool, together with Manchester, Birmingham, Glasgow and Belfast, as a major centre for the development of internal and European air services, and following extensive trials early in the year, on 18 May 1948 commissioned an American ground-controlled approach (GCA) radar system to provide landing guidance in bad weather. This supplemented the existing standard beam approach (SBA) radio beacon system (which was essentially the same as that installed before the war by Liverpool Corporation). The GCA, although primitive when compared to present-day radars, represented the latest in blind-landing aids, and Speke was only the third airport in the country to receive the equipment. Because radar approach techniques were so new, much flying training time was devoted by both civilian and military operators to practice radar approaches, bringing many unusual aircraft to the airfield circuit. In 1949, associated with the GCA installation, the Ministry commenced installation of the then equally new Calvert centre-line-and-bar two-colour approach lighting system on the approach to Runway 26. Again this installation was one of the first in the country.

The Merseyside Aero and Sports Organisation that had revived the pre-war Aero Club had only flown for a few months in 1946 before ceasing operations. The only aircraft based at Speke early in 1949 were two Percival Proctors of the Lancashire Aircraft Corporation from Blackpool. These aircraft were used for army co-operation flying (as targets for Territorial Army anti-aircraft units), a common task for flying clubs and small charter companies at the time. Lancashire Aircraft Corporation also planned to operate scheduled services under Associate Agreements from a number of provincial points to London (including Liverpool–London) but none of these flights were operated because of the short notice given of their approval, and with no certainty of renewal in later years.

However, three events did take place in 1949 that slightly redressed the rather bleak outlook. On 11 April, BEA commenced a Speke–Cardiff service, via optional stops at Hawarden and Valley. This route was flown by Rapides each weekday and had been introduced in response to pressure groups in Wales who had demanded an internal air

Avro XIX G-AHIK in Starways dark blue colours after its purchase from British European Airways, at Speke in 1950. (Phil Butler collection)

service linking north and south Wales. The service was suspended for the winter on 1 October. Later in 1949 the Blackpool-based charter company, Starways Ltd, which had been formed in the previous year with the prime aim of offering a charter service for the many showbusiness personalities starring in shows on Blackpool's Golden Mile, moved its operations to Speke after a Liverpool businessman and city councillor, F.H. Wilson, had taken a financial interest in the business. The original Starways aircraft, Percival Q.6 G-AFIX, was destroyed in an accident at Pwllheli (Broom Hall) in May, but was replaced by a leased Avro Anson. Thirdly, the Hooton Park-based Wirral Aero and Gliding Club, operated by Squadron Leader G.C. Wright's Wright Aviation Ltd, expanded its operations by starting a new Liverpool Flying School at Speke, based in the pre-war flying club hangar. The new club was opened on 5 November 1949 and shared its fleet of Austers and Miles Hawk Trainers with the Wirral club. During April 1950, Wright Aviation's activities were totally transferred from Hooton Park to Speke because of expanded RAF operations at Hooton.

During 1950, Starways consolidated its operations at Speke, taking over No.3 Hangar (later used by Vernair and the Cheshire Air Training School before being demolished in 2000). The company added to its fleet by the purchase of Gemini and Avro XIX aircraft. The main operations were pleasure flying and Army co-operation work, although the ex-BEA Avro XIXs had been bought for use on a Liverpool–London (Northolt) daily scheduled service which was licensed from 5 April 1950 until the end of the year. (The route was abandoned at the end of the summer season in September.) An application to fly a weekly Liverpool–Jersey service with the Ansons was refused since BEA considered that it was liable to divert traffic from their Manchester–Jersey route. On 17 October Starways received their first Douglas DC-3, which immediately went into service on charter operations.

A posed shot of Sikorsky S-51 helicopter G-AJOV of British European Airways, departing on a flight to Cardiff in 1950. (BEA)

BEA, having withdrawn their Liverpool–Cardiff Rapide service on 1949, made history on 1 June 1950 with the start of a helicopter service from Liverpool to Cardiff, flown by Sikorsky S-51s, with provision for an optional stop at Wrexham. This was the world's first sustained scheduled passenger service by helicopter, remaining in operation until 31 March 1951, by which time 819 passengers had been carried. Since at the time the flights constituted the main task of the BEA Experimental Helicopter Unit, the unit's maintenance base was moved from Yeovil to Speke in March 1950, and remained until the scheduled service was withdrawn.

1951 saw the arrival of Cambrian Air Services, which took over the Liverpool–Cardiff service from BEA, flying Rapides daily, starting on 7 April. The service connected with flights to Jersey at Cardiff, enabling through flights to be made on the service on weekdays. BEA itself commenced a Liverpool–Jersey direct service with Dakotas each Sunday during the summer.

While the operations described above were taking their course, the consequences of earlier retrenchment by BEA had filtered through to the Ministry of Civil Aviation. By this time Manchester Corporation had been lobbying for the development of Ringway, and although the total traffic figures still lagged behind Speke, various operations by major European airlines (such as Air France, KLM and Swissair) had been attracted to Manchester. Therefore, on 31 December 1950 the Liverpool GCA radar had been transferred to Manchester and twenty-four-hour operation of Liverpool Airport ceased shortly afterwards, since it was no longer equipped to receive bad-weather diversions.

Despite these setbacks, various other events were taking place regarding operations by independent airlines, and the operation of major airports. A change in government had helped to crystallise these changes, although it is likely that they would have occurred regardless of the politicians. From 1952 a new air-transport licensing process for scheduled services was introduced under the auspices of the Air Transport Advisory Council, which provided a body independent of BEA to determine more fairly the balance of interests between the state corporations and the independent (i.e. privately owned) airline operators. Also during 1952 the government announced that it was prepared to consider local involvement in the operation of airports.

The advent of the Air Transport Advisory Council (ATAC) allowed Starways to receive approval of an inclusive tour service from Liverpool to Lourdes that operated from June to September 1952. An earlier service had flown in 1951 under the old associate agreement system, again in conjunction with F.H. Wilson's Cathedral Touring Agency Ltd. Under the ATAC, longer-term licences became possible, and from 1953 a five-year licence was granted, enabling longer-term planning and

Ex-RAF Douglas Dakota G-AMPZ, with others, awaiting civilian conversion by Starways, April 1952. (R.A. Scholefield)

investment. Another feature of the ATAC regime was that an appeals procedure was available. Thus, when BEA planned to introduce a daily Liverpool–Jersey service for the 1952 season, Cambrian Air Services was able to object on the basis that their Liverpool–Cardiff route was only viable if empty seats were taken up by passengers flying on to Jersey. The appeal was successful, resulting in Cambrian receiving a five-year licence to fly from Liverpool to Cardiff, Guernsey and Jersey, and BEA's withdrawal from the route.

The greater licensing freedom also resulted in two competitors for BEA on the Liverpool–Isle of Man route for the 1952 summer season, with Starways using Dakotas and Manx Air Charters flying Rapides. During the whole of the post-war period to this point, Aer Lingus had used Dakotas on the Liverpool–Dublin service, but in 1952 the Bristol 170 Wayfarer was used on some flights. Four of these aircraft had been purchased in the expectation of a boom in air freight traffic, although in practice they were usually flown as mixed passenger/freight aircraft.

An Opportunity Missed?

As noted above, the new Conservative government had made policy statements regarding the participation of local authorities in the running of airports, which was a reversal of previous policy. Accordingly, on 28 November 1952, Liverpool Corporation representatives met Ministry of Civil Aviation officials in London to discuss the consequences of these changes, and soon afterwards a city council resolution was tabled, asking for a detailed report on the legal and financial position. The airport was then run by the Ministry of Civil Aviation under the requisition powers originating in 1939, although the ministry paid the corporation a rent of £13,000 per annum for the use of the land and facilities, as compensation for the requisition of the property.

After months of discussion, a report was presented to the city council on 29 April 1953, detailing three possible alternatives:

1. The airport might be purchased by the ministry at a price of £250,000. The compensation 'rent' would then cease.

2. The airport might be taken back by the corporation, on condition that it would continue to be run as a public-use aerodrome, in which case the ministry would transfer all assets created by the state to the corporation free of charge, would continue to provide all air traffic control and technical services free of charge for a period of twenty-one years, and would share capital expenditure on new developments with the corporation on a percentage basis to be agreed.

3. The ministry would continue to run the airport under its requisition powers, paying its compensation rent.

The options were discussed in the report with full details of the financial implications. Option 1 was financially advantageous, but meant permanent loss of control by the city. Option 2 meant an estimated loss of £54,000 per annum (a cost of two pence in the pound on the city rates), while Option 3, the status quo, meant a much smaller loss, because the ministry's rent payments balanced two-thirds of the loan repayments still outstanding on the corporation's pre-war capital spending. The report made no recommendation as to the course of action, but its closing words set the tone of the general view held at the time: 'The Committee will no doubt bear in mind that the two attempts in the post-war period to operate a London service have proved unsuccessful from the Operator's point of view.' This implied that the possible income from new air services would not be likely to reduce significantly the deficit on the city rates, because the public had not used services that had operated in the pre-war period. So the Airport Committee, and the city council, decided on the status quo, and the terms for the return of the airport to city control were declined.

Airwork

A minor event in the summer of 1952 was the use of the airport by a number of Supermarine Seafires, being ferried from RNAS Anthorn on the Solway Firth to Gatwick, where they were to be overhauled by Airwork General Trading Ltd for the Burmese government. On one occasion a Seafire became unserviceable and was hangared overnight in the otherwise empty No.1 Hangar. Perhaps the ferry pilot passed on this fact, because it was soon announced that Airwork was to rent the hangar for the overhaul of NATO fighter aircraft, the North American Sabre swept-wing fighter being mentioned. On 17 November 1952 the first three Sabres arrived from RCAF squadrons based at North Luffenham in Rutland. Over the following months a trickle of other Sabres arrived, but it was almost a year before the scale of work became obvious to the casual visitor. The initial overhaul work on Sabre Mk 2s was used to train the workforce before the operation got into full swing, which it began to do with the delivery of two Sabre Mk 4s on 9 October 1953.

The Canadair-built Mk 4 Sabre was that intended for service with the RAF, although the RCAF in Europe initially used many Mk 4s, pending the delivery of later versions to the Canadians. All the surviving Mk 4 Sabres used by the RCAF came to Airwork at Speke for maintenance and repainting prior to handover to the RAF. By the beginning of 1954 the Airwork hangar began to bulge at the seams and many aircraft could be seen parked outside awaiting attention; in earlier months the closed hangar doors hid all activity from view. By April 1954 sixty Sabres had arrived for overhaul prior to handover to the RAF, and the first few RAF Vampire NF.10 night fighters had arrived for modification to navigation trainer standard, the first such aircraft having flown in on 5 March. During the next fifteen months a total of thirty-six Vampires arrived for modification, the RAF Sabres gradually departed and, starting on 23 April 1954, a new batch of RCAF Sabre Mk 2s began to replace

DH Vampire night fighters awaiting attention at Airwork, with a Starways Dakota and an RCAF Sabre in the background, April 1954. (R.A. Scholefield)

them. The RCAF aircraft were now coming in to be overhauled prior to transfer to Greece or Turkey under Mutual Defence Aid arrangements; the final delivery of these aircraft was from another Airwork establishment which had in the meantime been set up at Ringway, so the aircraft were only quite rarely seen at Speke in Greek or Turkish colours. The Greek and Turkish aircraft totalled around fifty or so, dealt with between April 1954 and May 1955. From July 1955 to January 1958, the Speke base dealt with ex-RAF Sabre Mk 4s, this time being overhauled prior to transfer to Italy or Yugoslavia. In all cases these aircraft left Speke in American markings (but with their original Canadian serial numbers), since the USA was financing the transfer. About eighty ex-RAF Sabres were involved, although many more were dealt with at other locations. These were the main activities of the Airwork base at Speke, although there were others, including the major repair of RCAF Lockheed T-33s in 1955, the storage of a few Bristol 170s for their manufacturers in 1956–57, the overhaul of seven DH Doves for the Iraq Petroleum Co. in 1956–57 and, finally, the overhaul of two ex-RAF Dakotas for Sudan Airways in 1957–58.

The Airwork base closed in February 1958, after a bid to overhaul ex-RAF Lockheed Neptunes for delivery to Argentina was rejected and no other work could be found. Nevertheless, for over five years the company provided work and income for the area, as well as much to interest local aviation enthusiasts. At their peak, Airwork had space in Nos 1, 2 and 6 Hangars, and occupied the main No.1 Hangar throughout their period of residence, although a section was fenced off to provide space for the maintenance of the two Pionair-class Dakotas of BEA's Liverpool Flight.

Canadair Sabre Mk 4 XB618 at Speke in 1956. This was a jet fighter built in Canada (under licence from North American Aviation) for the Royal Air Force; after RAF service it was overhauled at Speke, painted in American markings and delivered to Yugoslavia. (Don Stephens)

Requisition Continued

For 1953, work had been authorised by the Ministry of Civil Aviation to widen and strengthen the apron and perimeter tracks, in preparation for BEA to reintroduce a London–Liverpool–Belfast service with Airspeed Ambassadors, but in the event the service did not start and the work was cancelled. The monotony of the BEA Dakotas on the Irish Sea routes was varied slightly by the use of Vickers Vikings on a few summer Isle of Man services, this being the London–Isle of Man aircraft employed during its scheduled stopover at Ronaldsway. Since 1951 the Dakotas had been the Pionair class, which were thirty-two seat conversions with built-in passenger steps, two-crew cockpit layout and distinguished by a colour scheme incorporating a white top to the fuselage. The pattern of the BEA Irish Sea routes remained essentially unchanged until 1 April 1960, when the Viscount 701 was introduced as a replacement for the Pionair. Similarly, the pattern of Aer Lingus operations continued with little change during the 1953–60 period, with frequencies varying from twice-daily Dakotas during the winter up to seven flights on a Saturday in summer, of which two or three might be inclusive tour operations during the later years. Although the Dakota (DC-3) was the mainstay of their operation, Bristol 170s were used on some flights between 1952 and 1955, and then on 15 December 1958 the first propjet Fokker Friendship appeared, gradually replacing the DC-3 from then on.

In 1953, Cambrian Air Services replaced their Rapides with the more modern DH Doves and the Jersey services developed so well that at the end of 1954 two

British European Airways Pionair-class Dakota in 1958. The Pionairs were refurbished Dakotas fitted out for two-pilot operation, with thirty-two passenger seats, integral passenger steps fitted into the rear door, and a white-top colour scheme. They served the Liverpool-based Irish Sea routes from 1951 to 1960. (Phil Butler)

Bristol 170 Wayfarer EI-AFQ of Aer Lingus *St Finnbarr* at Speke on 27 March 1954. These aircraft were bought in expectation of increasing freight traffic, but were usually flown as passenger aircraft. (A.M.G. Armstrong)

Cambrian Rapide G-AJCL on a charter flight in 1959, after being withdrawn from scheduled services, and in an uncharacteristic silver scheme with maroon markings; in earlier years the Rapides had been maroon overall. (Phil Butler)

Dakotas were acquired, followed in 1956 by three brand-new DH Herons, both the latter types being used on Liverpool flights according to traffic demand. In 1958 the airline sustained severe losses and the whole fleet was put up for sale at the end of the summer season. But for the intervention of BEA, with whom the airline had concluded an operating agreement in 1956, and which had taken a shareholding in the company earlier in 1958, Cambrian would have been forced into liquidation. However, operations restarted in 1959 using Dakotas leased from BEA, and the airline's fortunes recovered sufficiently for these aircraft to be purchased outright in 1960.

Before turning to a more detailed account of other companies that played a significant role in Speke's fortunes during the period to 1960, we will cover technical developments that took place in the 1953–60 period. The GCA had been transferred to Manchester at the end of 1950, leaving Speke with less sophisticated blind-landing aids – namely the standard beam approach installed before the war which was now becoming obsolete, and less accurate approach procedures based on the use of the non-directional beacon (NDB) installed on the approach to Runway 26, and the automatic VHF direction-finding equipment (VHF/DF). In 1954 it was announced that a new airfield control radar would be installed, and this entered service in the latter half of 1955 – this was the Decca 424 (later called a Plessey 424 after Plessey bought out Decca's radar business). This equipment had been developed to meet RAF requirements, but it was well suited to use at less busy civil airports, and the equipment

Cambrian Dove G-AJOT, in the earlier Cambrian Air Services colour scheme, in front of the terminal building. There are lots of empty spectators' seats on the balcony! (Phil Butler collection)

Cambrian Airways Heron G-AOGO awaiting departure to Jersey, probably taken in 1956. The colour scheme consisted of maroon cheatlines and titles with a Welsh dragon motif on the fuselage ahead of the Cambrian title. (Phil Butler)

installed was the first one sold for civilian application. The Ministry later bought similar radars for other airports where they operated the air traffic control facilities, and the same type was used at almost all other municipal airports in the UK.

By 1955, it had become obvious that the hastily laid wartime runways were in bad shape. For some years the Ministry had recognised the problem, but had reacted by notifying operators of runway strength limitations rather than spending money on maintenance – the runways were still adequate for Dakotas which could in any case be safely operated from a grass surface if need be. The Ministry planned for major resurfacing work that was duly carried out during 1956–57, causing the main runway to be closed for several months. A temporary grass runway was laid out parallel to the closed runway, on the terminal building side, with hardcore ramps to smooth out discontinuities in the surface, such as drainage paths at the edges of the other runways, while a flarepath of paraffin-filled 'goosenecks' was provided for night use. The work increased the load classification number of the main runway from LCN 12 to LCN 20, thus allowing regular operation by heavier aircraft such as the Viscount and Douglas DC-4. The final significant work undertaken during the Ministry's period of operation was during 1957–58, when structural alterations were made to the eastern wing of the terminal building, to provide passenger handling space in place of offices – a recognition of the demands of increasing summer traffic peaks brought about by inclusive tour flights.

Independent Airlines and General Aviation

Four companies that made contributions to the activities at Liverpool Airport during the 1953–60 period deserve detailed mention. The first three were separate entities but were nevertheless linked to one another by circumstances that will be described. The fourth company, Starways Ltd, played an important role that is covered separately below.

As mentioned earlier, Wright Aviation Ltd had set up a new Liverpool Flying School in 1949, and later moved completely to Speke, using the school aircraft for army co-operation flying and light charter work as well as school and club flying. By 1952 a Gemini and a Rapide had been added, primarily for charter work, and during 1953 a second Rapide had been leased from Starways. During the year an agreement had been reached for the operation of Anson freight aircraft for Mr Reginald J. Gates, a Liverpool businessman who was a prominent member of the flying club associated with the flying school. At this point Wright Aviation's financial backers withdrew their support in favour of a new operator called Dragon Airways that had been formed to operate a pleasure-flying contract at Pwllheli for the Butlin's holiday camp there. Wright Aviation was forced into liquidation and Dragon Airways took over its assets, including the operation of the flying school. The aircraft changed their colours from the yellow with red trim of Wright Aviation to the dark blue with white trim of Dragon. Dragon Airways Ltd was registered as a company on 16 January 1954, although their first Rapide had been delivered to Speke in September 1953.

A line-up of Wright Aviation aircraft, outside the aero club hangar in July 1953 – Rapides G-AHPT and G-AIBB, with Proctor G-AIAA of T. Wayman-Hales. G-AIBB is still in Starways silver scheme with blue trim, but Wright Aviation titles. (Phil Butler)

Some of the smaller Wright Aviation aircraft outside their hangar, also in July 1953 – Auster Autocrat G-AGVI, Auster J/4 G-AIPH and Miles Hawk Trainer G-ALOG, all in their cream colours, with red registrations and titles. The RAF ensign on the flagpole belonged to No.3 Port Squadron, RAFVR, based in the hangar in the background. (Phil Butler)

Another shot of Hawk Trainer G-ALOG in 1953. Liverpool Flying Club appears behind the cockpit, and the engine cowling legend is 'Wright Aviation Ltd. – School of Flying – Liverpool Airport'. (Phil Butler collection)

DH Rapide G-AKOB *Oboe Baker* of Dragon Airways, the first Dragon aircraft to arrive at Speke, in September 1953. The aircraft was painted dark blue, with a white roof and titles. (Phil Butler collection)

DH Heron 2 G-ANYJ *The Conqueror* of Dragon Airways, awaiting passengers in 1955, probably on a Liverpool-Glasgow service. Dragon Airways flew many services from Newcastle for the airline Hunting-Clan Air Transport, and the Hunting-Clan name appears above the entry door. At the end of 1955 Dragon's Liverpool base was shut and the airline moved to Newcastle. (Phil Butler)

Vickers Viking G-AOCH of Dragon Airways on a Paris-Liverpool-Newcastle service in July 1956, the last Dragon activity with a Speke connection. The service ceased at the end of the summer season. (Phil Butler)

Former Wright Aviation Auster J/4 G-AIPH, now in Dragon Airways blue colours in 1954. (Military Aircraft Photographs)

After Dragon Airways moved out in 1955, a new Merseyside & North Wales Flying Club was formed, using several ex-Dragon Airways Austers and other light aircraft. Here is Taylorcraft 'Plus D' G-AHAK in the club's overall red colour scheme with white markings. (Phil Butler collection)

Federated Air Transport Anson G-ALXC at Speke in 1958, in front of the Chapel House not long before that was demolished. The building to the right is No.35, one of the 1939 AAF hangars. (Phil Butler collection)

As well as continuing operations built up by Wright Aviation, including flying scholarship training for air cadets under contract to the Air Ministry, Dragon had ambitions to fly scheduled services and their first licences to fly from Manchester and Liverpool to Pwllheli were granted for the 1954 summer season, the Liverpool flights being operated by the DH Rapides used on pleasure flying for the Butlin's holiday camp at Pwllheli. For 1955, more ambitious plans were announced; three new DH Herons were ordered and a large network of services based on Liverpool and Stoke-on-Trent (Meir) were applied for. Of these, only those from Liverpool to Glasgow and from Stoke to the Isle of Man and Jersey were approved, the Liverpool–Glasgow route being inaugurated on 28 June 1955. A Liverpool–Paris route was later approved, but not immediately operated. Dragon had surplus capacity due to the refusal of licences applied for and this was utilised by flying routes from Newcastle on behalf of Hunting-Clan for which the Herons were more suitable than Hunting's own larger aircraft. The outcome was that Hunting-Clan bought out Dragon Airways and the company's base was moved to Newcastle on 1 November 1955.

During the 1956 summer season the Liverpool–Paris licence was used, when a newly purchased Vickers Viking inaugurated a twice-weekly Newcastle–Liverpool–Paris service, but the Liverpool–Glasgow service had been abandoned and in September 1956 the Paris service was also withdrawn, and all Dragon's connections with Liverpool ceased. The Liverpool Flying Club operation had in the meantime

Spitfire PS915 of the Temperature and Humidity (THUM) Flight, at Speke on 4 September 1954. For several years until 1957, Spitfires of this flight were daily visitors, handing their morning observations to the Meteorological Office in the terminal building for transmission to the main Met. Office at Bracknell. (Phil Butler)

Successors to the Spitfires of the THUM flight were de Havilland Mosquitoes, which continued the delivery of weather data to the Met. Office for three more years. (Phil Butler)

been taken over by Captain J. Green, a former Starways pilot, and was operated successfully for some years, until Captain Green was unfortunately drowned when a Tiger Moth owned by the club crashed in the River Mersey near the airport on 30 March 1958. The club, by then renamed the Merseyside and North Wales Flying Club, thereafter declined in its fortunes and expired totally with the departure of its last aircraft on 10 May 1962. Its successor, the present-day Keenair organisation, is covered later.

Mention was made earlier of Wright Aviation's intended operation of Avro Anson freighters for R.J. Gates in 1953. At the time of Wright Aviation's demise, Mr Gates had already signed contracts for the purchase of two Ansons from Transair Ltd of Croydon, but now had no operator to fly them. He therefore employed two ex-Wright Aviation pilots to set up an operation for him, and in late 1953 entered into business as the proprietor of Federated Air Transport. Its main task was to fly mushrooms from Ireland for distribution in the north of England by the Federated Fruit Company, Mr Gates' business in Liverpool. The operation had been offered to Dragon Airways, who spurned the offer as a non-starter, but in the event Federated Air Transport long outlived Dragon Airways. The fleet consisted of an ex-Starways DH Rapide as well as the two Ansons, and the entirely eastbound loads of mushrooms from Dublin to Liverpool were balanced by newspapers going in the opposite direction, or to the Isle of Man, and any other casual freight or occasional passenger loads which occurred from time to time. The company remained in business until February 1961, at which point new air transport licensing regulations were introduced which would have significantly increased the company's overheads if it had remained in operation, and it was closed in favour of using capacity on the Aer Lingus freight service from Dublin to Liverpool.

Starways

The early operations of Starways have already been covered up to 1952. Early in 1952, seven ex-RAF Dakotas were purchased to provide a more viable fleet, and the smaller aircraft were gradually disposed of, including two original Douglas DC-3s that had Wright R-1820 engines instead of the more common Pratt & Whitney R-1830 type. (The Wright engines suffered from problems in obtaining spare parts, so the ex-RAF aircraft were preferred.) The ex-RAF aircraft were gradually overhauled and put into service, or sold to other independent airlines. In 1953 the Liverpool–Isle of Man service was not operated, because a Glasgow–Isle of Man route was refused, and it was therefore not possible to co-ordinate these flights with intended Glasgow inclusive tour operations to Lourdes. The Lourdes operations, which had started at a single weekly flight, were now licensed at ten per week (including some flights from Glasgow, Manchester and other points in the UK). 1953 also saw the start of inclusive tour operations to Bilbao, thus breaking away from pilgrimage flights to a more general holiday tour operation; services to Bilbao, or to Biarritz in its place, continued for several years. In 1954, holiday flights to Nice were added, and an application was made to start a schedule from Liverpool to Heathrow. This route

A Liverpool City Airporter coach outside Lime Street railway station. This was one of a fleet of four coaches that provided a direct service to the airport from Lime Street and the Adelphi Hotel during the 1960s, replacing old Bedford coaches that had been acquired from British European Airways. (George Jones)

The 1938 terminal from a 'landside' aspect in the 1960s. (Austin J. Brown)

DH Fox Moth G-AOJH of Harry Paterson, another familiar sight of the early 1960s, awaiting pleasure-flight customers outside No.2 Hangar. The hangar was then in use by Cambrian Airways. (Phil Butler collection)

An apron scene from 1961, with a Starways Dakota, BEA Viscount 701, and a BKS Bristol 170 car-ferry taxiing out to take off for Dublin. (Phil Butler collection)

commenced in March 1955, initially at a frequency of three flights per week, but was built up over the following years to provide daily services with day-returns available in each direction. By 1958, seventy-two-seater Douglas DC-4s were used on some Heathrow services; the DC-4s started to join the fleet in September 1957, and had been acquired for an enlarged Lourdes 'pilgrimage' programme planned for the centenary year of the Lourdes shrine in 1958. Other inclusive tours operated by 1958 included services to Basle, Palma, Santander and San Sebastian, all on behalf of the Cathedral Touring Agency. In 1959, the Lourdes flights were run at a reduced level, but a new venture was a weekend-scheduled service from Liverpool to Newquay, inaugurated on 13 June by DC-4 G-APEZ. The success of this operation led to flights to Newquay from other cities in the following year. 1960 also saw the start of services from Liverpool to Ostend (weekly in the summer) and from Liverpool to Glasgow on weekdays from 12 October. Inclusive tour flights in 1960 operated to Tarbes (for Lourdes), Santander, Palma, Biarritz, Oporto, Rimini, Perpignan and Munich. The services had expanded from a total of fewer than 5,000 passengers in 1952 to almost 41,000 in 1960. This increase relied on the persistence of Starways in the face of route licensing policies that still favoured the state corporations, and other problems such as the restricted operational hours of the airport.

Starways' two Viscounts, G-APZB and G-ARIR, parked in front of No.2 Hangar, probably in 1962. (Phil Butler collection)

A Cambrian Viscount 701 on final approach to Runway 26, landing over Speke Hall Avenue, with the Calvert line and bar approach lighting stretching back towards the Metal Box works on Speke Road. (Phil Butler collection)

5

Back to Municipal Control

The hard work undertaken by Starways and to a lesser extent by Cambrian and other operators, together with plans announced by new airlines to come to Liverpool in 1959–60 (including BKS Air Transport, Dan-Air and Overseas Aviation) and a strong campaign in the local press in support of the airport, had changed the public perception of its value to the city in the years since 1953 when the city council had declined terms for its return to municipal control. The reason for the press campaign stemmed from another shift in government policy, in that it was proposed that the state would no longer own airports, and those under requisition would be returned to their previous owners by the end of 1960. Although the future of the airport still seemed in doubt, and a matter for public debate up to the moment of transfer, the council had accepted a willingness to negotiate transfer terms in January 1959, and the proposed terms were outlined by the Ministry of Aviation (successor to the Ministry of Transport and Civil Aviation) to the town clerk of Liverpool in November 1959. The terms included the free transfer of state assets in return for the corporation waiving claims arising from requisitioning, and that the ministry would provide air traffic control and technical services at its cost for seven years, providing that any extension of the airport's hours of operation would be subject to negotiation.

These terms were significantly worse than those on offer in 1952, in that there was no suggestion that the ministry would participate in the financing of capital development, and was unwilling to commit itself to any period greater than seven years for the provision of technical services. However, the town clerk's report was more optimistic on the prospects for reducing the operating deficit than that prepared seven years earlier. The report was accepted by the city council on 6 April 1960, and preparations went ahead for the city to resume responsibility for the airport from 1 January 1961.

The year 1960 also saw several developments that augured well for the future. These included:

1 April 1960   BEA introduced Viscount 701s on the Irish Sea routes in place of Dakotas. At first this resulted in sharply decreased frequencies, but the superior aircraft rapidly attracted more passengers, enabling frequencies to be restored in later seasons.

Dan-Air Dove G-AIWF, photographed in April 1960, shortly after the start of their Liverpool–Bristol service. (Phil Butler)

4 April 1960   Dan-Air started a Liverpool–Bristol service with DH Doves, the airline's first domestic scheduled service, initially operated three days per week.

25 April 1960   BKS Air Transport inaugurated a Liverpool–Dublin car ferry service, operated daily with Bristol 170s. In the peak season the frequency increased to four flights daily.

6 August 1960   Due to fog at Manchester, the Saturday night 'newspaper lift' to Dublin, flown by Aer Lingus, was operated from Speke. This led to the permanent transfer of the operation from Manchester to Liverpool from November 1960.

These events helped to create confidence in a successful future, and set the scene for the official transfer, which took place on schedule on 1 January 1961, with a formal ceremony following on 6 January. The passenger figures for 1960 had shown a significant increase, and those for 1961 produced a further increase of 42 per cent. The increase was partly due to a publicity campaign initiated by the airport director, Wing Commander H.W.G. Andrews, partly a boom in the local economy (arising from the arrival of the Ford Motor Company and other new businesses in the area), and partly the increasing use of more pressurised, turbine-powered aircraft. Starways introduced their first Viscount into service on 10 June.

Dan-Air meanwhile extended their Bristol–Liverpool route to Newcastle on 4 January, and used Dakotas in place of the Doves on some flights from 6 July. The year 1962 saw the start of a Dan-Air Liverpool–Rotterdam route on 9 January. This was transferred to Amsterdam on 4 October 1965. In later years the Amsterdam route was served by Ambassadors, then by Comets, before reverting to HS.748s. An Amsterdam flight was the last Dan-Air service to fly from Liverpool, being withdrawn in 1975 at the time of a fuel crisis and doubts on the future of the airport. Liverpool was omitted from the 'Link-City' (which by then encompassed Newcastle, Manchester, Birmingham and Bournemouth) during 1974.

A BEA Birmingham–Liverpool–Belfast service operated by Viscount 800s started on 1 April 1962. This re-established separate morning departures to the Isle of Man and Belfast that had been abandoned when the Dakotas were first replaced by Viscounts. Euravia Ltd started an inclusive tour to Valencia on 20 May, using a Lockheed L.049 Constellation, the first inclusive tour flown from Liverpool by a company other than Starways and Aer Lingus.

New Facilities

The first few years of corporation operation continued to show a trend towards new services and expanding traffic. One of the first tasks undertaken by Wing Commander Andrews was a review of the facilities to identify ways to stimulate new traffic. This resulted in work costing £400,000, which was largely complete by June 1962. The most significant items in this programme were:

1. Extension of Runway 08/26 by 500ft to the west, bringing its length to 5,627ft.
2. Extensive resurfacing of the existing runways, taxiways and aprons to increase their load classification number (LCN), thus allowing unlimited operations by most types of airliner in service.
3. Construction of new taxiways parallel to Runway 08/26 to give wider and straighter routes, widening those sections of the existing taxiways remaining in use and installing centre-line lighting.
4. Installing visual approach slope indicators on Runway 08 to compensate for the lack of approach lighting on that runway.

At the same time it was announced that £213,000 would be spent on improvements to the terminal building and that various schemes were under consideration to provide a runway of 7,000 feet in length.

By 1963 the decision had been taken to build an entirely new runway on land to the east of Speke Hall, between Hale Road and the River Mersey, to be linked to the existing runways by a taxiway crossing National Trust land adjacent to Speke Hall. Consideration had been given to extending the existing runway 08/26, either across Speke Hall Avenue towards Speke Road, or by a programme of tipping into the Mersey at the river end of the runway. The former was not favoured because rising ground in the approach would have allowed most of the extension to be used for take-off only, while the latter was rejected because a shipping channel would have been affected by the tipping.

British Eagle Viscount G-AMOC, photographed in 1964 wearing Starways titles, which were used on a small number of Viscounts before the company changed its name to British Eagle (Liverpool) Ltd. (Phil Butler collection)

British Eagle Britannia G-AOVS, photographed in September 1965, awaiting passengers to London (Heathrow). (Phil Butler)

Liverpool Aero Club Piper Colt G-ARKN, photographed on the western apron in June 1964. This was one of four Colts flown by Jim Keen's newly formed Liverpool Aero Club, which developed into Keenair and the present Liverpool Flying School. (Phil Butler)

Cambrian Dakota G-AHCZ, an ex-BEA aircraft, pictured at Speke some time after BEA had taken a financial interest in Cambrian. (George Jones)

Agreement to cross the Speke Hall land was reached on the basis that an embankment would be provided at the corporation's expense to protect the Hall from noise and vibration, and that the land would be returned to the National Trust if it ceased to be used for access between the two airfield sites. Tenders for the runway work were sought in September 1964 and work started on in November. The new runway design incorporated the latest thinking of the International Civil Aviation Organisation, the United Nations agency concerned with establishing standards for civil aviation throughout the world, and complied with the requirements of ICAO's Annex 14 specification that came into force in August 1964. The specification laid down more stringent requirements for runway gradients, and those of surrounding land. The runway was built by G. Percy Trentham Ltd at a tendered price of £2,314,258, while Campbell & Isherwood Ltd received a contract for the electrical work at a price of £750,000. Initially the runway was to be 7,000ft long, although this was revised to 7,500ft at an early stage. The runway was 150ft wide with 25ft hard shoulders at each side, and had a parallel taxiway along its whole length, attached to a link connecting the new system to the old airfield. The runway had taxiway loops at each end and high-speed turnoffs for each landing direction. The main structure was concrete, although the runway had a 'friction coat' of specially graded tarmac over most of its length to allow water drainage and thereby prevent aquaplaning. The runway was also provided with extensive lighting set into

British Eagle DC-4 G-ASPM in August 1964. This was one of two bought by British Eagle to fly inclusive tour flights that had been originally booked for Starways DC-4s. (Ian Keast)

Aer Lingus Carvair EI-AMP at Speke in 1964 operating a car ferry service to Dublin. (Don Stephens)

Cambrian Viscount 701 G-AMOA in British Air Services' colour scheme in August 1969. British Air Services included the former Cambrian Airways and Northeast Airlines regional operations, but was later completely absorbed into British Airways. (Don Stephens)

The newly complete 'new' runway in 1966, at that time designated 10/28. It is now 09/27, due to the variation of magnetic north occurring in the meantime. (The numbers come from the directions of the runways in tens of degrees, measured from magnetic north.) (Liverpool Airport)

its surface and 1,000 yards of approach lighting at each end. The lights at the river end were installed on gantries built in the river. The work also included installing a full instrument landing system on the landward approach, building a meteorological observation building to the south of the runway and an extension of 1,000ft at the river end of the short 17/35 runway on the old airfield, resurfacing the old 04/22 runway (disused since 1959) for use as 'the central taxiway', and building new parking bays as an extension to the existing main apron in front of the old terminal building. The runway was opened by the Duke of Edinburgh on 7 May 1966, and remains in use as the runway at the new airport site. The runway was designed to accept unlimited operations of almost all types of aircraft from a weight point of view. The ILS was designed to be a Category II installation – that is, to be suffi-ciently accurate and with sufficient back-up systems (runway and approach lighting and guaranteed power supplies) to be used in conditions of 400m horizontal and 100ft vertical visibility. In practice much development work was needed, and it was not until 21 July 1969 that the installation was notified as being approved for Category II use. It had been used as a Category I system in the meantime.

It had always been intended that new ground facilities, including a new control tower and separate terminal building, would be provided adjacent to the new runway, and the plans announced in 1963 envisaged that a further £3 million would be spent on such facilities.

Progress Continues

The year 1963 opened with BEA operating the Irish Sea routes, using Viscount 700s to the Isle of Man and Viscount 800s on the Birmingham–Liverpool–Belfast day return service, which was showing significant increases in traffic. The BKS car ferry had been withdrawn in 1961 because of the severe financial difficulties of the airline, and a planned takeover of the route by Channel Airways, another British independent airline, had not taken place. However, in 1963, Aer Lingus (which had introduced Fokker F-27 Friendships on their passenger service in 1958, and also used Viscounts in busy periods) reopened the car ferry service, having purchased two Aviation Traders Carvairs to fly this and a number of other car ferry and freight services. The first flight was on 8 May 1963 and the route was operated until 1965, when the B&I shipping line introduced drive-on car ferry ships on its routes between the UK and Ireland. In 1964 Aer Lingus operated three car ferry flights daily with the Carvairs, together with twenty-seven passenger services each week by Friendship or Viscount, and three inclusive tour flights per week by Friendship.

Cambrian Airways operated to the Channel Islands, including a limited service during the winter months, still using Dakotas. However, big changes were to occur during the year, and on 1 April 1963 Cambrian Airways took over all the Irish Sea routes, using a fleet of Viscount 701s transferred from BEA. Euravia operated inclusive tour flights with Constellations (for Universal Sky Tours) from 12 May.

Meanwhile, on 2 March 1963, Piper Colt G-ARGO was delivered from Kidlington, this being the first aircraft of the new Liverpool Flying School started by Jim Keen, which gradually built up its operations over the following years. At first the aircraft were hangared in No.39 Hangar, but later No.4 Hangar was taken over and was used until 2000 when the business was transferred to the south airfield site.

Starways still operated the London service with Viscounts, DC-4s and Dakotas, some flights being via Chester (Hawarden), while the Glasgow service operated twice each weekday, via Blackpool, using Dakotas. Seasonal scheduled services flew to Newquay, Cork, Ostend and Dinard, and there was a large number of inclusive tour flights, by this time operated for Arrowsmith Holidays and YTC Universal Ltd, in addition to the Cathedral Touring Agency. At the end of 1963, a major event took place that was to have a significant effect on the airport's fortunes. On 19 November an agreement was signed between Starways Ltd and British Eagle that resulted in a takeover of Starways with effect from 1 January 1964. The Starways fleet remained with the original directors of Starways, who formed a new company called Aviation Overhauls Ltd to lease out these aircraft to other operators, and to carry out maintenance work on these and other aircraft. This work was concentrated on the new hangar (No.85) which had been built by Starways to the east of No.2 Hangar on the Speke Road frontage, and which had been in use since 1958. Two other hangars were still under construction at the time of the takeover, these also being on the Speke Road frontage, further to the east. These buildings had been intended as an extension of Starways' maintenance base, but were never used as such. They were mostly used for storage or industrial purposes, apart from a period when one was used by Dan-Air for line maintenance on their based Ambassadors (used on a Liverpool–Amsterdam service, and for inclusive tours).

British Eagle took over space in No.1 Hangar for their line maintenance work, and later occupied the whole hangar for use as a subsidiary engineering base to their main base at Heathrow, which could not easily be expanded and was being fully utilised. From 1 January 1964, the London service became a completely propjet operation, with Viscounts on three services per day, one of which flew via Hawarden, and a Bristol Britannia operating the first northbound service in the morning and then returning to London. Two Eagle Viscounts received Starways titles, but otherwise remained in the British Eagle colour scheme. The Glasgow service was also operated by Viscounts, twice daily in each direction, the former stop at Blackpool being omitted. The summer timetable included an increased London service, with two Britannia flights per day in addition to the Viscounts, with two flights a week each to Ostend, Newquay and Cork, also by Viscount. An average of nine inclusive tour flights per week were also flown for the Cathedral Touring Agency, Arrowsmith and YTC Universal, using either Viscounts or two DC-4s which had been bought solely for these services. Eagle's DC-4 and Viscount maintenance was concentrated at Speke, under the auspices of British Eagle (Liverpool) Ltd, to which Starways changed its name on 1 August 1964.

For 1964, Cambrian Airways flew ten times a week to Guernsey and Jersey, as well as operating the Irish Sea routes to Belfast and the Isle of Man. A number of the Belfast flights originated at Cardiff, while one flight each day on the Isle of Man route continued to Heathrow. The London service had been licensed in competition with Starways, although it had only come into operation a short time before the Eagle takeover. All Cambrian services were by Viscount apart from four of the Channel Islands flights that were still by Dakota. New services for 1964 were by Mercury Airlines, from Liverpool to the Isle of Wight on Saturdays, and Manchester–Liverpool–Exeter on Sundays, using Herons, and occasionally a Dakota when bookings were heavy. In addition to the British Eagle-operated inclusive tours, Euravia expanded their flights to Valencia, Palma and Perpignan. Euravia had been negotiating to set up their engineering base in No.1 Hangar, but were pre-empted by the arrival of British Eagle. Perhaps because of the failure to establish their base at Liverpool, Euravia withdrew to Manchester for the 1965 season.

The year 1965 saw a similar pattern to the scheduled services, although Eagle's London service had increased from twenty-seven to thirty-nine flights weekly, and new Liverpool–Manchester–Rimini and Liverpool–Birmingham–Palma routes were opened. Cambrian had joined in to compete with Eagle on the Cork route, each airline flying three services per week, and in November opened a twice-nightly cargo service to Belfast. Aer Lingus had reduced their car ferry to two flights per day, but had increased their passenger services. The main Cathedral/Arrowsmith inclusive tour programme was flown by Canadair Argonauts of British Midland. A new tour operator, Gaytours of Blackpool, flew Autair Ambassadors to Pisa and Barcelona. The 1966 season followed the pattern of the previous year once again, with the Eagle Liverpool–London service now at forty-four flights per week, and the introduction of an Eagle Liverpool–Dublin service on six days per week. The Aer Lingus car ferries had been withdrawn, but Carvairs were still used on weekday cargo services, while the Friendships had been retired in favour of an enlarged Viscount fleet, at a reduced frequency. Cambrian now operated a daily Isle of Man freighter in addition to the Belfast freight flights. Inclusive tours were operated by British Midland, Autair, Dan-Air, British Eagle and Aer Lingus. A new inclusive tour operator was Schreiner Airways, flying Friendships for Hards Travel, to connect with coach tours at Amsterdam.

From 18 July 1966, the airport returned to 24-hour operation, after long, painstaking negotiations with the ministry, considerably easing the operation of inclusive tour and night freight flights. With the introduction of the winter schedules, after intermittent use since July, British Eagle timetabled BAC 1-11 jets on the London route in place of Britannias. The Dublin service was withdrawn in 1967 because of Eagle's inability to agree timetables with Aer Lingus. Otherwise, Eagle Liverpool services were little changed from the previous season. Cambrian and Aer Lingus services were unchanged, except that Viscount freighters had replaced the Carvairs. The inclusive tour operations for 1967 involved seven flights per week by Britannias and Viscounts of Treffield International, a new airline formed to operate inclusive tour services, with a few other flights by British Eagle, Invicta, British Midland, Dan-Air and Aer Lingus, for the usual agencies. A new operation was an inclusive tour to Munich, flown by Bavaria Flug with BAC 1-11s.

Top: British Eagle BAC 1-11 G-ATPH *Salute.* This was the first regularly scheduled jet aircraft type to fly from Liverpool. (Phil Butler collection)

Middle: Cambrian BAC 1-11 G-AWBL. The only pure jet aircraft used by Cambrian on scheduled and inclusive tour services from Liverpool. (Phil Butler collection)

Bottom: Cambrian Viscount 806 G-AOYI. This is an example of the larger Viscount 800s that took over from the earlier Viscount 700s on Cambrian services. (Phil Butler collection)

In the event, Treffield International failed to establish itself and its operations ceased on 23 June 1967. A rescue operation for Treffield passengers was mounted by British Eagle, which took over most of their services, albeit at a more realistic price to the travel agents. This in turn resulted in the liquidation of YTC Universal Ltd at the end of the season, thereby reducing the consortium of Liverpool tour agencies that had supported the tours flown by Starways, British Eagle and others to two (Cathedral Touring Agency and Arrowsmith Holidays). The 1967–68 winter timetable saw the opening of a Liverpool–Manchester–Frankfurt route by British Eagle using BAC 1-11s each weekday. During 1967 the British Eagle base had begun to carry out Britannia maintenance work, following modifications to No.1 Hangar which had taken place in 1966; an extra bay had been added to the western side of the hangar to enable the fins of large aircraft to be accommodated. In 1968 the routine Britannia work was extended to include major modifications, converting passenger aircraft to have large freight doors.

The 1968 summer season saw the British Eagle London service cut back to thirty-five flights per week, because of the 1967 electrification of the Liverpool–Euston railway line. The much-improved rail service provided severe competition for the airlines and a cutback in capacity was inevitable. Because this service was the most popular passenger route flown from Liverpool, the setback had a noticeable effect on the total passenger figures. The remaining Eagle routes were little changed, although there were no services to Dublin, Cork or Ostend. The Liverpool–Birmingham–Palma service was flown three times weekly with BAC 1-11s, while a new licence allowed a weekly flight to Ibiza, also via Birmingham.

Meanwhile Cambrian operated thirteen flights per week to the Channel Islands, twenty-six to the Isle of Man and fourteen to Belfast (six via the Isle of Man). The Cork service still operated on three days per week, but now operated via Manchester, while Cambrian had gained daily flights to Dublin at the expense of British Eagle. There were six freighters per week to the Isle of Man and seventeen to Belfast. Aer Lingus operated twenty flights per week to and from Dublin. A new scheduled operator for 1968 was Channel Airways, which inaugurated a Liverpool–East Midlands–Southend route on 17 June with Viscounts or HS.748s. This operated twice each weekday, one flight also calling at London (Stansted). Interline arrangements were made with Cambrian to offer connections with the Irish Sea routes. Channel Airways continued their Southend–East Midlands–Liverpool operation until June 1969. The service was poorly patronised, but by 1969 Channel were hoping to take over Eagle's Liverpool licences and in January 1969 commenced an ambitious 'bus-stop' service from Southend to Aberdeen via seven other airports, which connected with the Liverpool service. The service was withdrawn in June after the airline failed to secure other established routes from Liverpool, although inclusive tour operations for Cathedral continued for the rest of the summer season. In November 1969 Skyways commenced a contract service between Stansted and Liverpool with HS.748s on three days per week, operating for the Ford Motor Company, who had been a major user of the Channel Airways service. This service continued for several years until Ford substituted its own Gulfstream I in place of the chartered aircraft.

Because of the introduction of a £50 foreign travel expenditure limit by the government, inclusive tour flights were severely cut, the main programme for Cathedral Touring Agency and Arrowsmith being only four flights per week by Laker Britannias and BAC 1-11s, plus one flight each by British Eagle and Channel. Aer Lingus had two inclusive tour flights per week, while the Bavaria Flug flight to Munich continued. With the introduction of the winter timetable, the Newcastle-based airline BKS appeared at Liverpool again, this time routing Leeds–Belfast passenger flights via Liverpool on four days per week, the first such service being flown by Viscount G-AOYH on 4 November 1968. The winter Leeds–Liverpool–Belfast link continued until BKS (later renamed Northeast) and Cambrian were merged into British Airways in 1976.

The most significant event of 1968, however, happened two days later, when it was announced that British Eagle International Airlines was ceasing operations. Although British Eagle (Liverpool) Ltd was a separate company, all aircraft used on its services were owned by BEIA, so perforce its operations also ceased. Although over the next few months efforts were made to revive British Eagle (Liverpool) Ltd, none of these passed the scrutiny of the Air Transport Licensing Board, and the airline went into liquidation along with its parent. At the time of the collapse, four BEIA Britannias, a BAC 1-11 and a Viscount were grounded at Liverpool and remained until flown out on the liquidator's instructions.

The use of Liverpool as a base by British Eagle had put the city and its airport on the map. Although the British Eagle operations had a solid foundation built up by Starways, the Eagle ethos had developed the services in a very professional way. In particular this had been shown on the London route, where traffic had trebled (and even after rail electrification, it was still double that of Starways). The resources of a large airline had made available flexible responses to changes in traffic demand, and provided modern equipment and professional expertise. A competitive spirit had been developed that encouraged a healthy response from other airlines such as Cambrian, resulting in benefits for the competitors and the Liverpool travelling public as well as for British Eagle. New routes had been opened to Rimini, Palma and Ibiza, which had been dismissed as 'non-starters' even by others in the travel and airline business, but had proved to be well patronised by the public. The collapse of British Eagle came as a shock, but immediate problems were solved by allowing Cambrian to operate the London and Glasgow services without a licence, pending a hearing of various applications for the routes. The only applicant for all of the British Eagle licences was Channel Airways, and Channel would only have operated them if it had been granted the whole network (which did not come to pass). The airport authorities gave their support to Channel only on services not applied for by Cambrian, not wishing to place all their eggs in one basket. In practice, this ensured that Cambrian received the profitable London and slightly loss-making Glasgow routes, while the peripheral routes were granted to Channel. Without a base operation the holiday routes by themselves became unprofitable and were never operated by Channel Airways.

Retrenchment

From 1969 onwards the plans for the terminal alongside the new runway were taken down and dusted off from time to time, but the will to stand the capital expenditure was not there, for very understandable reasons:

1. British Eagle, or an equivalent operator willing to promote Liverpool air services, was not there.
2. Other regional airports such as Manchester and Birmingham had received government money to fund capital developments, thus enabling them to see the prospect of losses on their own outlay being recovered in a reasonable period of time, but this assistance was never offered to Liverpool.

Therefore, from this point, although money was spent on various developments, these were of a short-term nature. For example, No.2 Hangar, which had been Cambrian's line maintenance base while Eagle occupied No.1 Hangar, was converted to an international arrivals and departures building to relieve congestion in the main terminal. Despite the erosion of confidence arising from the demise of British Eagle, traffic still showed a rising trend. After an initial dip in figures in 1968–69 due to the effect of London rail service improvements, traffic rose again in 1970, to reach a peak in 1973.

Political developments during the period caused difficulties for the airport, with the very real possibility of complete closure hanging over it for some years, due to changes in the political control of Liverpool City Council that produced various examples of 'instant' decisions to save ratepayers' money, regardless of the long-term consequences. The passenger traffic decreased from 1974 to 1977, directly or indirectly because of uncertainty about the airport's future. Scheduled services that were withdrawn during the fuel crisis were not all restored thereafter because of the uncertainty, and in 1977 there was also a national firefighters' strike that stopped airline services for six weeks. The closure threat was probably at its peak early in 1974, shortly after the reorganisation of local government, and there is absolutely no doubt that the threat resulted in a failure to attract new traffic and contributed to a withdrawal of several of the existing services, including the Dan-Air 'Link-City' routes and the Thomson inclusive tour programme. The fuel crisis of the following year resulted in suspension of all services for several weeks, after which the Glasgow and Amsterdam routes were never restored. In 1978 traffic started to rise again, until 1981 when a recession started to bite. The peak figure of 600,026 terminal passengers in 1979 was much inflated by a night runway closure at Manchester that brought many extra flights to Liverpool, while the 1980 figure was also inflated to some extent by the same phenomenon.

A major change during the late 1960s was the development in 'general aviation' – i.e. club flying, executive aircraft and charter work by small aircraft. The two main companies in the field at Speke were Keenair, which had grown from Jim Keen's Liverpool Flying School started in 1963, and Vernair, a subsidiary of Vernons football pools organisation, registered in 1967. Keenair Services was launched on 17 September 1968 and commenced charter operations with a Piper Apache. In

1974 an Aztec replaced the Apache, and further aircraft were later added. The Keenair operations were closely integrated with those of the flying school, which over the years flew mostly Piper aircraft. The exceptions were vintage aircraft, of which there was almost always one in the fleet for Jim Keen's personal use. Vernair was formed in 1967, and originally employed a Beech Queenair for the use of Vernons' executives. British Eagle serviced the Queenair, but after Eagle's collapse, Vernair set up its own maintenance organisation in No.3 Hangar, and expanded into specialist charter work and aircraft maintenance. In 1975 the charter work started to include the operation of regular flights from Liverpool to Thurso for the UK Atomic Energy Authority. The company continued to operate from Liverpool for some years, but was eventually taken over by Northern Executive Aviation Ltd at Manchester, with all operations being transferred there in March 1987. A further general aviation operation worthy of mention was the Cheshire Air Training School, which moved to Speke in June 1970, shortly after its formation. The school remains at Liverpool, flying Cessna 150 and 172 aircraft.

As mentioned earlier, Cambrian Airways had taken over the London and Glasgow services immediately after the collapse of Eagle in 1968, flying seventeen Viscounts per week to Heathrow in addition to the existing daily Isle of Man–Liverpool–London flights. The Glasgow route was served by ten rotations per week, Dublin by five, and Jersey three during the winter season (the Jersey routes flying via Manchester, Bristol and Cardiff). From January 1970, Cambrian began to use BAC 1-11s on some Heathrow services, and by the summer timetables Cambrian were operating BAC 1-11s on most London and Dublin services. Because the jets were used, services via Hawarden had been abandoned, and the Cork route had also been withdrawn. Cambrian operated most of the inclusive tour flights from Liverpool in 1970, with seven BAC 1-11 and two Viscounts per week. For the winter, Dublin services reverted to Viscounts.

Due to further runway repairs at Manchester, the Aer Lingus cargo service terminated at Liverpool for the winter instead of continuing to Ringway, and a number of Manchester flights by BEA and Dan-Air operated to Liverpool during the same period. Aer Lingus withdrew their Viscount cargo service, following the introduction of Boeing 737s in passenger/cargo configuration on the evening Dublin–Liverpool service from 1 April 1970. From then most Aer Lingus flights were by 737s or BAC 1-11s.

1970 was particularly noteworthy for the number of ad hoc freight charter flights operated for the Ford Motor Company, resulting in the year's freight tonnage breaking all previous records, at 19,912 tons. Over 300 Ford flights by Dakota-sized aircraft or larger were made during 1970. Ford had often used freight charters, but 1970 was an exceptional year. In 1970 Britannia operated a weekly 737 to Palma, and a fortnightly service to Munich with Britannias. Inclusive tour services in 1971 were significantly increased in number, with Cambrian flying thirteen or fourteen flights each week and Britannia Airways operating a further three. A new service, of interest because it was the first 'third-level' schedule to be started from Liverpool, commenced on 29 June 1971, with Air Anglia Islander G-AXVP flying from and to

Piper Aztec G-BCPF of Keenair Services Ltd in November 1975. In the background is the Keenair (No.4) Hangar and the wooden annexe alongside that was for many years the Liverpool Flying School premises, adjoining the western apron. (Phil Butler)

Cheshire Air Training School Cessna 150, with its Cheshire Cat tail logo, also on the western apron in November 1975. The hangars behind show the Keenair and Vernair titles. (Phil Butler)

Norwich. This service was flown twice a week and it was later routed via Manchester in both directions. The service continued in 1972, but was withdrawn at the end of the summer. The winter schedules were similar to the previous year except that Cambrian operated inclusive tour flights to Palma. Overall, 1971 was a good year, with total passengers exceeding the half-million mark for the first time. The 1971 summer had seen an almost identical scheduled service pattern to the previous year, although in fact there were more seats on offer because Cambrian were replacing their Viscount 700s with the larger 800s and used BAC 1-11s on a few more flights. 1972 and 1973 repeated the pattern of the previous years.

Inclusive tour flights were reduced in 1972 in comparison to the previous year, with an identical Britannia programme, using 737s on all flights (707s had flown to Palma in 1971), and the Cambrian programme reduced to nine flights per week. Despite reductions in inclusive tours and scheduled flights to Dublin, traffic continued to increase. A significant event on 20 November 1972 was the arrival of a Laker Airways DC-10 on a demonstration flight to travel agents – the first wide-bodied jet to visit Liverpool. Inclusive tour flights for 1973 increased slightly, Cambrian operating eleven and Britannia four flights per week. The Munich inclusive tour used British Airways Vanguards instead of Bavaria 1-11s. Record passenger figures were recorded, with a total of 586,723, while freight figures approached the record level of 1970.

Cambrian Airways had many critics, and maybe operated without the style and flair of British Eagle. That being said, Cambrian did not let chances pass them by, a prime example being the operation of night freighter services to the Isle of Man and Belfast. These were mainly, but not exclusively, flown to carry newspapers that had previously been flown from Manchester by BEA. Cambrian were also alive to the development of inclusive tour routes that provided fuller use of their fleet, and in the last years of their separate existence their own agency, Cambrian Air Holidays, extended its programme to include Liverpool. As the years went by the ability of the Cambrian management to operate independently became restricted. The pattern of services in 1974 was similar to the previous year, but passengers and the number of flights dropped almost to 1971 levels. By then the remorseless amalgamation of Cambrian Airways into British Airways was taking effect, and the ability of its directors to take independent action was constantly diminishing. The Cambrian newspaper flights to Belfast ceased in March 1975, and although 1976 saw a repeat of the schedule pattern established in 1975, Cambrian Airways disappeared as a name on 31 March 1976 and its services continued under British Airways' name. Cambrian Air Holidays' inclusive tour flights for the 1976 season were operated by Laker 1-11s, Aviaco DC-9s and JAT Caravelles at fifteen flights per fortnight. Cambrian Air Holidays then disappeared from the scene.

After a month of ad hoc charter flights by Alidair and Air Bridge Carriers (ABC) in place of Cambrian, a contract was granted to Alidair to fly newspapers from Liverpool to Belfast on six nights per week from 1 May 1975, using Viscounts. On 23 February 1976, ABC took over the Belfast newspaper flights from Alidair, using Argosy freighters; from 3 April this operation included Saturday flights previously operated by Cambrian. Another operation started in 1975 was by Eli Lilly, the pharmaceutical firm, with its own Boeing 707, carrying goods from the Dista factory in Speke; the first flight was on 14 April. The 707 usually arrived from Gander and returned to the US via Shannon or Basle, where it loaded items from other factories. Flights ceased in 1977 after seventy had been made.

6

Merseyside County Council Development

The new Merseyside County Council had supported the airport as a necessary facility for the region, and took over interim responsibility for it in 1974. A protracted series of negotiations then ensued that eventually confirmed the county's responsibility for the airport in 1977. The city council remained the landowner, and received rent from the county. Although the convolutions of local government meant that Liverpool remained the largest source of county council funds, in future the financial burden of the airport was shared with the other Merseyside boroughs, so that Liverpool paid 44 per cent of the costs to the county, instead of bearing 100 per cent itself.

By July 1977 it was announced that improvements would be made to the terminal building and this work was carried out during the winter season. All did not go well at first, because it was announced that ABC had lost the Belfast newspaper contract from 31 October. The lack of night flights forced the withdrawal of 24-hour operation to save costs. Other freight flights were in decline, with the end of Eli Lilly flights and the withdrawal of Aer Lingus' combined passenger/freight services in favour of using passenger aircraft. Other problems, including air traffic controllers' and firemen's strikes, caused disruption to scheduled services during the year. On the plus side, a highlight was an influx of football supporters on 16 March (for a Liverpool v. St Etienne game), which gave Liverpool Airport its busiest day ever. The loss of newspaper flights was short lived; the operator that had taken over did not operate successfully and ABC regained the contract. Initially, ABC flew from Manchester, but returned to Liverpool in March 1978 when 24-hour operation was restored. 1978 brought increases in traffic. Representations made to British Airways resulted in increased London and Isle of Man services, the London service in particular having been eroded over the previous few years. Laker and Britannia flew the usual inclusive tours. During 1978 negotiations were in progress between British Airways and British Midland about an exchange of routes, which resulted in British Airways pulling out of Liverpool and taking over some BMA services out of Birmingham. The transfer took place on 29 October and resulted in an immediate increase in services, including five daily DC-9 flights to Heathrow, and the inauguration of a Liverpool–East Midlands–Brussels–Frankfurt route. The

Irish Sea routes were maintained at three flights daily to Belfast and the Isle of Man, and a daily Dublin service. These services continued for the 1979 summer season, together with a five times weekly Jersey service. Ironically, within days of British Airways' departure, the airline provided Liverpool with its first Boeing 747 visit on 10 November 1978 when G-AWNI diverted to Liverpool en route from Bermuda to Heathrow with 393 passengers on board.

The inclusive tour programme for 1979 included flights by British Midland, Laker, Aviogenex, TAROM, Britannia and Transeuropa, together with various flights transferred from Manchester because of the nightly closure of Manchester's runway for reconstruction. This work also brought in Aer Lingus, KLM, Swissair and Lufthansa freight services for the whole of the 1979 summer season. While the Manchester closure traffic boosted both passenger and freight statistics to record levels, 1979 was also significant because of the first Post Office night-mail services on 2 July. These flights quickly grew and became an important operation for the airport. The first trial flights were from Glasgow, Newcastle and Bristol, but the success of the scheme was quickly proved, and by the end of July a Norwich link had been added and in August one to Gatwick. Mail was also carried on the ABC freighter to Belfast. By September a sorting office had been built to support the operation. 1979 also saw the first flights of the 'Guppy' that ferried Airbus wings from Chester to Bremen for completion. A trial was successfully made on 8 July 1979, and, although the main operation remained at Manchester, a number of flights used Liverpool in 1979, 1980 and 1982. The first Concorde to visit Liverpool was Air France's F-BTSC on 26 August 1979, the first Concorde charter operation from a UK regional airport.

In 1980 as in 1979, Manchester was closed during the night for a period for further runway work, and the Swissair, KLM, Lufthansa and Aer Lingus freight services again operated from Liverpool, together with a large number of diverted flights. Liverpool's own inclusive tours had declined substantially, with flights only by Aviogenex and British Midland. BMA's London service reverted to Viscounts in place of DC-9s in October and the Brussels/Frankfurt and Dublin services had been dropped in March. 1981 saw the start of a number of 'third-level' services using the Embraer Bandeirante. Air Ecosse opened the first of these on 30 March between Liverpool and Aberdeen. Also, Genair became established at Liverpool, starting a Liverpool–Gatwick route on 3 August. Over the coming months Genair introduced further services, but the airline was later taken over and its route network shut down on 13 July 1984. Finally, on 14 December 1981, Jersey European Airways commenced a twice-daily Liverpool–Dublin service – by this time the Aer Lingus service had been reduced to one flight per day. British Midland continued the Heathrow service with Viscounts, but introduced Friendships in their place in November. The Jersey route continued, using the DC-9, although an inclusive tour operation by British Air Ferries also flew to Jersey. Other inclusive tours included Aviogenex to Pula, Aviaco to Palma and Malaga and TAP to Faro. By this time inclusive tours from Liverpool were in decline because major tour operators were unwilling to provide services.

The temporary control tower erected in 1982 for International Aeradio when they took over air traffic control services from the CAA. This was located near the western end of the south airfield, and was used for a few months before the permanent control tower was completed. (Phil Butler)

The Irish Sea routes had never been routinely profitable for any operator, largely because of a combination of short flight times and extreme variations in seasonal demand. This led to discussions between the owners of the operators to the Isle of Man (British Midland and British Island Airways) about the rationalisation of their routes and resources. Out of these discussions arose the formation of Manx Airlines on 1 November 1982, as part of the British Midland group, to take over routes formerly operated by British Midland and BIA between England, Belfast and the Isle of Man.

Development Work

By this time, Merseyside County Council had decided that it was necessary to bite the bullet and to plan for the transfer of airport operations to the new runway site, and work had proceeded to fence off the landside areas and to provide services to the site. The plan was to proceed in phases, with the first comprising a new control tower and rescue services building at a cost of £1.86 million. Work on the new tower started on 23 March 1982, and was completed with a 'topping-out' ceremony on 24 November. At the same time, the council had invited tenders for the operation of air traffic services. Tenders were received from the CAA (the existing provider) and International Aeradio Ltd. The latter won the work, and took over on 1 April 1982,

British Midland DC-9-15 *Dovedale* in April 1982, after British Midland had taken over the former British Airways' services from Liverpool in 1978. (Gerry Manning)

Vernair King-Air G-VRES photographed in June 1981, the flagship of the Vernons' executive aircraft fleet that was based in No.3 Hangar from 1968 to 1986. (Gerry Manning)

Opposite: A busy day again, one of the busiest at the old terminal site, when St Etienne football supporters arrived in a large fleet of charter aircraft to visit Anfield on 16 March 1977, with Caravelles parked on the short 17/35 runway. The shot shows the apron extensions built in 1966, and the wartime 'temporary' steel hangars built around No.1 and beyond, in the Banks Lane area. (Liverpool Airport)

initially using a temporary ATC building erected on the new runway site (from this time normally called the south airfield, or the new Liverpool Airport). The Phase 1 work included installing a new instrument landing system for Runway 27 and a Plessey ACR430 radar to cover both approaches to the new runway. At this time the old 08/26 runway was closed, although runway 17/35 stayed in use for mail aircraft until the new Mail Centre opened.

Phase 2 of the new development started on 28 January 1983, when the first sod was cut for the new parking apron, complete with taxiway and floodlighting, service roads and security fencing. Three-quarters of the cost of £1.4 million for the 33,000m² apron and £400,000 for ancillary works was met by the Department of the Environment, the first central government aid for capital works ever granted, although over £500,000 for Phase 1 had come from the European Economic Development Fund. Concurrent with the apron work, the Post Office funded the construction of a sorting office adjacent to the apron to support the night mail operation. The mail centre came into operation on 9 January 1984.

Phase 3 of the work was delayed for some time by the failure of Liverpool District Council to designate the area as an Enterprise Zone to qualify for more European funding. Phase 3 eventually went ahead, and included a design and build project (after selection from several tenders) for the construction of a new passenger

Another aerial shot taken in the summer of 1973, showing the old and new airport sites with the link taxiways, the eastward extension of runway 26/08 built in 1963, together with the new taxiways parallel to that runway built at the same time. (Liverpool Airport)

terminal. Wimpey Construction started work on the building on 25 February 1985. The influence of central government was still felt, because its approval was still required for the county's share of the funding, and this resulted in some scaling down of the terminal. Other portions of Phase 3 included the other work necessary in order to be able to transfer aircraft operations from the north airfield, including roads, car parks, and a fuel farm that was opened on 19 November 1985. The new terminal came into operation on 28 April 1986, by which time Merseyside County Council had been dismantled, an event that caused further fluctuations in the fortunes of the airport.

The Conservative government had decreed, by the enactment of the 1986 Airports Act, that limited liability companies must in future operate municipal airports having a turnover of greater than £1 million per annum. This was a problem, because in 1986 the airport still made a substantial loss, and following the closure of Merseyside County Council there was no immediate prospect of a company being formed. The airport was handed over to the Merseyside Passenger Transport Authority while negotiations took place to set up a company. The interlude of MPTA operation was not a happy one, since the authority focused on bus and rail functions rather than on the airport.

The control tower built for Merseyside County Council on the southern airfield, as part of Stage 1 of the progressive development at the new runway site. This shot shows the building nearing completion in 1982. (K. Sharp)

The 1986 terminal building erected by Merseyside County Council, and opened as the county council itself was being disbanded. The building, called a 'cowshed' by some, actually served well – with various changes over its life – until it was swallowed up in the new 2002 terminal built for Liverpool Airport PLC. (Adrian Thompson)

Air Route Changes

British Midland withdrew from the Heathrow route in April 1986, and the service was taken over by Manx Airlines, using Short SD.3-60s or a Saab 340. However, Manx struggled to run a service that attracted popular support, and British Midland returned to the route on 31 October 1988, using Douglas DC-9 jets. The service was withdrawn on 28 March 1992, because BMA wished to use the Heathrow slots for more profitable routes from London to Europe. British Midland continued to fly the seasonal Liverpool–Jersey route to the end of the 2001 season. Various attempts were made to reopen services to London in the intervening period, the most notable being those to London City flown by VLM (4.1.94–12.11.94), and the Luton route flown by easyJet from October 1999 until March 2001.

On 26 May 1988 the Irish low-cost carrier Ryanair commenced a Dublin–Liverpool service in competition with Aer Lingus Commuter. This service did well and, following a reallocation of routes between the two airlines by the Irish government, Aer Lingus withdrew from the Liverpool route on 15 January 1990. Ryanair has since continued to fly the services to Dublin. Also in 1988 (on 6 February), the express parcels company TNT commenced a nightly freight operation, initially to Cologne. This was later transferred to Liège when this replaced Cologne as the main European hub of the TNT operation. Although this service has recently been reduced because of a different pattern of car-part carrying to and from Merseyside factories, it continues to be an important nightly operation.

In June 1993, another freight operator, Emerald Airways (originally operating as Janes Aviation), transferred its operations to Liverpool. A number of its freight flights across the Irish Sea had flown from Blackpool, but the 24-hour operation of Liverpool Airport made these operations more viable than from Blackpool. Emerald flew an extensive network of mail, express parcel and newspaper flights across the Irish Sea or as part of the nightly Royal Mail flights from Liverpool. In April 1996 Emerald Airways started up a competitive passenger service to the Isle of Man, which ran until 1999, and led to greatly increased carryings to the island. However, in 1999 Emerald decided to withdraw from passenger operations. The freight and mail operations continued from Liverpool and other bases until 2006, and the Isle of Man passenger operations were restarted for a period in 2004–05 with BAe ATP aircraft.

In 1994, the airport was able to attract Bond Helicopters to Liverpool, to fly support flights to oil and gas rigs under construction in the Irish Sea for Hamilton Oil. These flights commenced on 10 August 1994, and resulted in the construction of a hangar and dedicated helicopter terminal that came into operation during March 1995. The Bond flights moved away to Blackpool during December 1998, when the requirement for 24-hour rig support was no longer needed.

Manx Airlines continued to operate the Liverpool–Isle of Man service, although ownership changed in the meantime, and the airline became associated with (and finally absorbed into) British Airways. On 9 January 1995, the Liverpool–Belfast route, which had also been operated by Manx Airlines, was transferred to British Airways Express, a franchise operation spun off from Manx. This route continued until May 2001, when it was withdrawn in the face of competition from easyJet. During February 2002, it was announced that Manx Airlines would lose its identity, but the Manx dimension would be maintained with the registration in the island of British Airways CitiExpress (Isle of Man) Ltd as the licensed operator of the routes. However, the overall operation has become indistinguishable from any other run by British Airways.

The significant turning point in the airport's fortunes came about in 1997, with the announcement that the low-cost airline easyJet that operated at Luton was to commence flights from Liverpool on 26 October. These started with daily Boeing 737s flying to Amsterdam and Nice. The services proved to be successful, enabling new routes to Geneva and Barcelona to start in January 1999. The trend continued with Belfast and Malaga flights in July 1999, Madrid in September and Palma in October. The routes have expanded so that over 1.4 million passengers flew on them during 2001. EasyJet and the airport signed a twenty-year agreement in October 2000 based on the proposition that expansion would continue, and that seven Boeing 737s would be based there by 2003. During March 2002, Paris services were announced (to start on 2 May 2002), together with expansion of existing Belfast, Palma and Nice routes. In January 2003, a further new route, to Alicante, was added.

The strategy of attracting low-cost airlines was confirmed by the announcement in January 2002 that Ryanair (who continue to fly the Liverpool–Dublin route) would start a Liverpool–Brussels service in June 2002, and would develop other routes to set up a 'hub' of services by the airline, with aircraft based at Liverpool, although, at the time of writing only the Brussels (Charleroi) service is operating.

7

The Public Limited Company

The company, Liverpool Airport PLC, was set up on 31 March 1988 and took over responsibility for the operation of the airport on the following day; the company was jointly owned by the five Merseyside local authorities (Liverpool, Wirral, Sefton, Knowsley and St Helens). The funding of the company was guaranteed by the councils, to the extent of £9 million by Liverpool, £4 million each from Sefton and Wirral, and £3 million each from Knowsley and St Helens. During the year, the freehold of all the airport land was also transferred from Liverpool City Council to the airport company. From this point, the airport was at last set upon a course where it could survive relatively independently of national or local politics. Of course, at the time, the local authorities still provided the working capital for operations and development and shouldered the operating losses. Within the constraints of spending by a loss-making operation, small developments continued, with the resurfacing of the runway in 1987, the construction of a bonded store to support the airport's duty-free shop, and the construction of a freight shed by the British Midland group, which came into operation in 1990.

The next major development was the purchase of a 76 per cent controlling interest in the airport company by British Aerospace, which took effect on 1 June 1990. This change was perhaps seen by some, with unreasonable expectations of instant trans-formation into an era of dramatic traffic growth and profitability, as being a 'false dawn'. BAe's involvement stemmed from the appointment of Chris Preece as the managing director of Liverpool Airport PLC in October 1988. Soon after joining the company he had presented a case that promoted BAe involvement, based on the proposition that Liverpool Airport was a prime site for further development as part of the UK's air transport infrastructure. At the time BAe had extensive property development interests and their financial interest in the airport company blended well with their property portfolio, thus giving rise to the purchase. For some time afterwards, while some capital was invested in a major apron extension (operational in September 1991) and in improvements to the terminal building, significant efforts were expended in developing an ambitious scheme involving land reclamation from the Mersey and the construction of a parallel runway, with possible associations with the then-proposed Mersey Barrage. Whilst this proposal was counter-productive both in terms of public perception of the airport and the use of scarce resources, it led in December 1993 to a more modest set of proposals upon which BAe based their well-argued case for the development of Liverpool instead of the construction of a second runway at Manchester. These plans involved a realignment of the main runway to decrease the environmental impact of the air traffic using the airport, and increasing the capacity of the terminals to take 12 million passengers per annum.

In December 1994 a Scottish-based holiday company, Direct Holidays, announced that it would start operations from Liverpool on 1 April 1995. This was a major coup for the airport, providing a substantial tour operator willing to initiate a large-scale operation based on flights from Liverpool. Although the company was later to be taken over by Airtours PLC, Liverpool has continued to be a major centre of the company's activities, and has proved to be a highly successful operation that has also resulted in several competitors initiating or restarting Liverpool-based holiday flights. Thomson Holidays returned in 1998, while Airtours itself restarted operations in 1999. The same year saw a major new operation by First Choice, and a smaller one by JMC commenced in 2002.

The end result of the 1995 public inquiry was the approval of Manchester's second runway, but the planning enquiry that considered the conflicting Liverpool and Manchester proposals was a much closer-run thing than might have been expected at the start, and it did a great deal to raise the profile of Liverpool Airport to previously unimagined heights. Even though the argument over the runway was 'lost', one result was the return of significant inclusive tour traffic (described above), which might not have happened but for the British Aerospace advocacy for Liverpool's case. While BAe sought to sell their holding following the Manchester second runway inquiry, at a time when they were seeking to reduce their property interests, it is a credit to their own efforts in raising awareness of Liverpool Airport's value that they were able to find such a willing and committed purchaser as Peel Holdings when the time came. In this they were of course aided by the steady growth in air travel that has continued over the years, and significant improvements in local road infrastructure (particularly the M57 extension in April 1996), but it is doubtful if these favourable trends alone would have had such an effect so quickly without the BAe input. The transfer from British Aerospace to Peel Holdings took place in July 1997, since when the airport has gone from strength to strength. Peel Holdings finally bought out the minority local government interests in the airport company in May 2001.

The Peel investments in the airport started to show in September 1998, when work started on a major (15,000m^2) extension to the main parking apron, and the start of work on four new hangars in the following month that were completed during 1999. In the meantime a new surveillance radar (a Marconi S511) had been installed to replace the older Plessey equipment. In September 2000 construction of a new control tower commenced on the south side of the runway, slightly outside the airport boundary, and this came into full use in January 2002. In conjunction with the new tower, the radar facility was upgraded to incorporate a secondary surveillance facility for the first time. Also on the technical side, on 17 April 2003

Left: Another airside view, this time of the Liverpool Airport terminal opened by HM the Queen in 2002. This shows the building with some modifications made during 2003, and with the nearest of the row of hangars to the right. (Dave Graham)

Right: A landside view of the impressive 2002 terminal, showing the Liverpool John Lennon Airport title. (Dave Graham)

a second instrument landing system (ILS) was brought into use (on Runway 09), supplementing the one that had previously been installed on Runway 27 many years before.

General aviation, which for many years has been a strong supporter and user of the airport facilities, has not been neglected. A new general aviation parking apron was constructed during the winter of 1998–99 and finally came into operation in September 1999. Keenair, the oldest of the local general aviation operators, was the first to build a hangar adjacent to the new facilities, and this came into use in August 2000, enabling the final complete closure of facilities on the old north airfield on 29 August. Keenair operates the Liverpool Flying School, aircraft engineering and charter services, and also on 26 May 2000 started a scheduled service between Liverpool and Cork, flying EMB-110 Bandeirantes. Ravenair, a company that had previously operated at Manchester Airport and moved to Liverpool in June 1998, has also built its own hangar, which came into use in January 2002. Ravenair has the concession for handling all general aviation aircraft using Liverpool and has a large fleet of training and light charter aircraft, as well as providing engineering and handling services.

Another milestone was the announcement in July 2001 that the airport would be renamed Liverpool John Lennon Airport, honouring one of Liverpool's best-known personalities. Although this move still arouses some controversy, there is no doubt that it was an astute move in the marketing of the airport to a wider public audience. The renaming was announced in a ceremony attended by Yoko Ono, John Lennon's widow, on 2 July 2001, and was further confirmed by the unveiling of a statue of John Lennon by Yoko Ono in the new terminal building on 15 March 2002.

The biggest of the new investments in Liverpool Airport has been in the £32.5-million new passenger terminal, the first phase of which came into use in January

HM the Queen at the official opening of the new terminal building on 25 July 2002, alongside the commemorative plaque, with Robert Hough (chairman of Liverpool Airport PLC). (Liverpool John Lennon Airport)

2002. This engulfed the 1986 terminal building, which has effectively been incorporated within the new building. The original plan announced in September 1999 was for an entirely separate building to be built to the west of the present terminal area, but this was changed due to the urgency of providing facilities for the ever-expanding easyJet flights. The current phase of the building is designed to handle 3 million passengers per annum, but planning permission has been sought and approved for further westward extensions to enable this figure to be increased to 4.5 million in due course. The seal of approval on the new terminal building was its official opening on 25 July 2002 by Her Majesty the Queen. The 'low-cost air travel' strategy certainly justifies the bold investment policies initiated by Peel Holdings, by which mass air travel is allied to a high-quality airport and ground transport infrastructure. This author hopes and expects their faith in the future to be justified, and wishes them well for that future.

The developments continued during 2003, with the confirmation that the next stage of development, to handle 4.5 million passengers per year, would proceed, with further extension of the terminal building, car parks, landside roads and aircraft parking areas. As with the earlier work on the new terminal building, this project was partly funded by the Objective One funding from the European Union allocated to the Merseyside region.

8

The Low-Cost Revolution

The previous edition of this book, *Liverpool Airport – An Illustrated History* was published in 2004, and since then the development of the airport's facilities has continued apace, to mirror the consistent growth of passenger traffic, primarily – but not exclusively – generated by the 'lo-co' (low-cost) airlines. The market leaders in this sector are certainly easyJet and Ryanair, the two airlines that now provide the majority of services from Liverpool John Lennon Airport, but the Hungarian carrier Wizz Air is another significant operator. At the end of 2003, easyJet was flying scheduled services to ten destinations and based seven Boeing 737 aircraft at Liverpool, since replaced by eight Airbus A319s. Their rival, Ryanair, although it had flown Liverpool–Dublin services for a number of years, was testing the market with a daily return flight to Charleroi (marketed in typical Ryanair fashion as 'Brussels-South'). Their subsequent service to Gerona was the first of many new routes established by Ryanair since that time, with more than thirty destinations now served from Liverpool, and the likelihood of further expansion yet to come. The network of flights operated by easyJet has also expanded, so that their operation at the time of writing is of comparable size, catering for approximately two million passengers each year. While easyJet fly to fewer destinations than Ryanair, easyJet's Liverpool–Belfast route is flown with up to seven rotations per day, making it the busiest air route within the UK other than those originating at one of the London airports. It is likely that Ryanair, which in 2007 flew comparable numbers of passengers from and to Liverpool to the easyJet totals, will overtake easyJet in total numbers.

easyJet

To recap on the last edition, the start of the 'low-cost revolution' came with the arrival of easyJet as an operator from Liverpool in 1997. EasyJet had been started by the innovator Stelios Haji-Ioannou in 1995, operating flights from Luton to Glasgow and Edinburgh, and had been courted by Liverpool Airport from the earliest days of easyJet's operation. This resulted in easyJet announcing in 1997 that it would start services from Liverpool and these flights, to Amsterdam and Nice, opened on

26 October of that year. The success of the two routes encouraged the airline to start further services to Geneva and Barcelona in January 1999. The flights to Geneva are normally flown by easyJet Switzerland, which is a subsidiary company. The year of 1999 saw further route expansion to Belfast and Malaga in July, Madrid in September and Palma in October. By October 2000 the airline and Liverpool Airport had signed a twenty-year cooperation agreement, based on further expansion of services and an undertaking that seven aircraft would be based at Liverpool by 2003. The aircraft used were initially Boeing 737-300s, which from August 2001 were gradually replaced by the more modern 737-700 series as the −300 versions were disposed of. EasyJet then ordered a large fleet of Airbus A319 156-seat aircraft to supplement and eventually replace the Boeing fleet. The Liverpool base started to receive A319 flights in June 2006, with the last of the based 737s departing on 25 November 2006. Boeing 737s from other easyJet bases continue to fly some services to and through Liverpool.

EasyJet's operations from Liverpool continue to be very successful. The Liverpool-Belfast service (which flies to Belfast International Airport at Aldergrove) is the busiest internal air route within the UK other than those that start or terminate at a London airport. Competing routes from Liverpool to the Belfast City Airport, arguably a more convenient location for travellers to or from Northern Ireland, have so far failed to make much of an impression on this operation. The coverage of their route network is shown in a table showing destinations and the start-date for their various routes. The main disappointment, perhaps, has been the abandonment of the Liverpool–Luton service, which provided cheap competition with the rail services between Liverpool and London. This service commenced on 1 October 1999, but was withdrawn on 24 March 2001. The reason for withdrawal was stated to be the 'low financial yield', but conspiracy theorists believe that contacts between Richard Branson (i.e. Virgin Rail) and Stelios Haji-Ioannou may have had something to do with it. Some other services have not survived – flights to Marseilles were withdrawn after a short time, with the capacity transferred to expansion of Polish routes, and it seems likely that flights to Cologne may be withdrawn during 2008 to allow aircraft to be used for flights to Innsbruck instead, but this possibility remains to be confirmed as this is written. One known adition for 2008 is a daily return flight to Jersey.

Destination	Start date	Typical flight frequency	Notes
Amsterdam	27.10.97	Three daily flights	(1st destination)
Nice	31.10.97	Twice daily	
Geneva	7.1.99	Daily	Extras in ski season
Barcelona	8.1.99		Twice daily
Belfast International	15.7.99	Six or seven daily	2nd aircraft based
Malaga	15.7.99	Three daily	
Madrid	6.9.99	Daily	3rd aircraft based
Luton	1.10.99	Three daily	4th aircraft based, withdrawn 24.3.01
Palma	26.3.00	Three daily	
Paris	2.5.02	Twice daily	

Destination	Start date	Typical flight frequency	Notes
Alicante	7.1.03	Daily	
Basle	28.3.04	Daily	
Berlin	28.4.04	Daily	
Cologne	22.6.04	Six per week	
Ibiza (seasonal)	24.7.05	Four per week	Peak summer only
Marseilles	11.4.06	Three per week	Abandoned 28.10.06
Faro	11.4.06	Daily	
Krakow	10.4.06	Daily	
Mahon (seasonal)	22.7.06	Twice per week	Peak summer only
Lisbon	2.11.07	Four per week	
Innsbruck	8.1.08	Three per week	
Jersey	31.3.08	Daily	

Ryanair

Ryanair started operations in 1985 as a small (one-aircraft) full-service airline, trying to offer competition to the Irish national airline, Aer Lingus Teoranta. In its early years it had its 'ups and downs', but survived because the Irish Government of the day supported the idea of competition and at a crucial moment decreed that Ryanair be given exclusive traffic rights on some of the cross-Channel routes from Dublin to the UK, including that between Liverpool and Dublin. Ryanair had started flying on the Liverpool route on 26 May 1988 and from January 1990 Aer Lingus withdrew from the route, resuming it for a time from 2004 to 2006 after Ryanair's exclusivity rights had expired.

During the 1990s Ryanair began to remodel itself in line with the philosophy of the US operator, Southwest Airlines, the successful low-cost carrier, rigorously cutting its costs. With the liberalisation of air traffic within the European Union in 1997, which did away with bureaucratic government controls on when and where airlines could operate within Europe, its dramatic expansion began. Originally this was based on operating a fleet of old, second-hand Boeing 737-200 series aircraft, but as the company became more established (and profitable) it was able to order a large fleet of brand-new Boeing 737-800 series aircraft in a standardised configuration with 189 passenger seats. So far as Liverpool was concerned, the last operation of the old 737-200 was on the Dublin route on 30 March 2005. In January 2002 Ryanair announced that it would start a daily service on the Liverpool–Brussels route. In true Ryanair style, the Brussels terminal was 'Brussels-South' at Charleroi, not the original overcrowded Brussels Airport at Zaventem. The route commenced on 27 June 2002 and was operated until 14 January 2004 when it was withdrawn, probably because of 'low-yields', although there were also other constraints on Charleroi operations at the time. This withdrawal was very disappointing, but no sooner was it announced but Ryanair stated that they would start a daily Liverpool-Gerona service on 5 February 2004 – and they have never looked back since.

In November 2004 Ryanair announced that they would open a permanent base at Liverpool, with four 737-800 aircraft based there, to come into operation from

31 March 2005. The first two based aircraft would fly to Murcia and Venice, while services to Rome and Milan/Bergamo were started a little earlier by aircraft from those bases. A third aircraft arrived to start flights to Limoges, Nimes and Reus on 18 April, and the fourth came to commence Cork, Pisa and Granada routes from 25 April, while flights to Shannon started on 3 May. The first expansion of the base took place with the arrival of the fifth aircraft on 26 September 2005 to commence the Oslo and Riga routes, and, in February 2006, Bergerac, Derry and Carcassonne routes. The next expansion of the base occurred with the arrival of the sixth and seventh aircraft from October 2006 to enable routes to Aberdeen, Alghero, Ancona, Grenoble, Inverness, Kaunas, Krakow, Poznan, Salzburg, Santander, Santiago de Compostela and Tampere to start. The complete list of Ryanair services appears below, with start dates and indicative frequencies. Some of these more recent routes may well not last; those to Aberdeen and Inverness having already been suspended from late 2007, while others are intended to be (or to become) seasonal in nature – for example, Grenoble and Salzburg are winter-only ski destinations. Nearly all of Ryanair's services have been resounding successes, but the airline, as personified by Michael O'Leary (its chief executive), does not suffer fools gladly. Any attempt by an airport to increase the airline's fees may well find that its Ryanair services cease or are drastically cut back. An example was Ryanair's operations on the Cork–Liverpool route, where several weekly rotations were transferred from Cork to Kerry for some months until the parties were once more 'on speaking terms'. Similarly, the daily routes to Aberdeen and Inverness, since abandoned, probably relied on temporary 'start-up' funding from sources in Scotland.

Although Ryanair has not attempted to go seriously 'head-to-head' in competition with easyJet, they now both operate in parallel to Alicante, Krakow and Palma, and will soon do so to Madrid. Also Ryanair will attempt to dilute easyJet's Belfast traffic (flown from Belfast International at Aldergrove) by introducing twice daily flights

The irrepressible Michael O'Leary, the Ryanair chief executive, in demonstrative mood at the announcement of Ryanair's Liverpool base in November 2004. (Liverpool John Lennon Airport)

between Liverpool and Belfast City Airport in 2007. Expansion towards the end of 2007 saw new routes to Stockholm, Budapest, Bydgoszcz (Poland), Fuerteventura, Lodz, Tenerife, Valencia and Friedrichshafen, some of them at the expense of existing destinations, which may be abandoned or become seasonal operations instead of all-year services. The last round of new services will not add to the existing seven based aircraft, but a substantial number of the new flights will be flown by aircraft based at the new destinations, rather than by the Liverpool-based fleet. The airport authority seeks to encourage this trend in order to level out the peak of early morning departures, which tend to overload the terminal facilities and cause problems with overnight aircraft parking arrangements.

A complete list of the services that have been operated by Ryanair appears in the table below, showing destinations, start dates and typical frequencies of operation.

Destination	Start date	Typical flight frequency	Notes
Dublin	26.5.88	Three times daily	
Charleroi	27.6.02	Daily	Ceased 14.1.04
Gerona	5.2.04	Daily	
Rome	28.1.05	Twice daily	
Milan/Bergamo	25.2.05	Six weekly	
Murcia	31.3.05	Daily	
Venice/Treviso	31.3.05	Daily	
Limoges	19.4.05	Four weekly	
Reus	19.4.05	Daily	
Nimes	20.4.05	Four weekly	
Shannon	3.5.05	Daily	
Cork	26.4.05	Daily	
Granada	26.4.05	Four weekly	
Pisa	26.4.05	Three weekly	
Oslo/Torp	27.9.05	Four weekly	
Riga	27.9.05	Daily	
Derry	9.2.06	Daily	
Bergerac	9.2.06	Three weekly	Summer only
Carcassonne	9.2.06	Four weekly	
Porto	23.2.06	Three weekly	
Seville	22.2.06	Two weekly	
Kerry	13.6.06	Three weekly	Ceased 13.1.07
Aberdeen	3.10.06	Initially daily	Suspended 2.11.07
Ancona	3.10.06	Three weekly	
Inverness	3.10.06	Initially daily	Suspended 2.11.07
Poznan	4.10.06	Three weekly	
Santander	4.10.06	Three weekly	
Santiago de Compostela	5.10.06	Three weekly	
Wroclaw	5.10.06	Three weekly	

Destination	Start date	Typical flight frequency	Notes
Kaunas	5.10.06	Three weekly	Suspended 8.11.07
Tampere	5.10.06	Four weekly	Winter only
Alghero	6.10.06	Three weekly	
Krakow	6.10.06	Three weekly	
Grenoble	21.12.06	One weekly	Winter only
Salzburg	21.12.06	One weekly	Winter only
Alicante	19.4.07	Daily	
Palma	27.3.07	Three weekly	
Bydgoszcz	28.10.07	Twice weekly	
Lodz	29.10.07	Twice weekly	
Fuerteventura	30.10.07	Three weekly	
Belfast Harbour	30.10.07	Twice daily	
Tenerife	30.10.07	Three weekly	
Madrid	30.10.07	Three weekly	
Stockholm (Skavasta)	31.10.07	Four weekly	
Budapest	31.10.07	Four weekly	
Valencia	31.10.07	Four weekly	
Friedrichshafen	22.12.07	One weekly	Winter only

Wizz Air

A further substantial 'lo-co' is the Hungarian company Wizz Air, which flies routes from bases in Central Europe, mainly former Eastern bloc countries. The company's first flights to Liverpool were from Budapest (soon withdrawn), Warsaw and Katowice, but it has since added ones to Gdansk, and the three destinations in Poland continue to be popular, with gradually increasing frequency of services. Most of the airline's flights to the UK operate to and from Poland, although it also started a route between Liverpool and Bucharest in Romania later in 2007. The frequencies of Wizz Air's flights on its Liverpool services have slowly but steadily increased.

The seven based Boeing 737-800s of Ryanair, taken before their early morning departures. A VLM Fokker 50 is also in the shot. (Adrian Thompson)

Destination	Start Date	Typical frequency	Notes
Budapest	7.12.04	Twice weekly	Ceased 26.3.05
Warsaw	7.12.04	Six weekly	
Katowice	7.12.04	Four weekly	
Gdansk	2.3.06	Five weekly	
Bucharest	1.10.07	Twice weekly	

Apart from FlyBe, whose operations are covered in the following chapter, the final 'low-cost' operator has been the Scottish-based airline, FlyGlobespan. This operator has flown with some success from its bases at Glasgow and Edinburgh, and announced services from Liverpool to Tenerife-South, to start on 1 November 2006. This was operated but capacity was eventually shared with Stansted, resulting in a poorer service (via Stansted) than (say) a direct flight from Manchester. The flight was withdrawn on 30 March 2007, and an advertised service to Prague was never started.

Subsequently, daily Boeing 757 flights from Liverpool to Newark, New Jersey, were announced on Independence Day 2006, to start on 25 May 2007, with the US terminal later being transferred to New York's Kennedy Airport. This service started, but was dogged with aircraft technical problems, exacerbated by lack of back-up aircraft resulting in much adverse publicity. Also, most flights operated via Knock in Ireland, a fact that greatly extended the flight time in both directions, and was not advertised initially to people who had already booked to fly from Liverpool. This did not bode well for the success of the service. Although a provisional timetable was published for the continuation of this service into 2008, it seems certain to be abandoned after October 2007. A weekly service to Hamilton, Ontario (for Toronto), was also announced by the airline and commenced on 25 May 2007. The Hamilton flights were flown with much better regularity than those to New York and appear to have been well patronised. It remains to be seen whether this service will return in 2008.

Seven of the easyJet Airbus A.319s based at Liverpool. Most easyJet flights operate from the 'Tango' parking stands to the east side of the terminal building. (Adrian Thompson)

9

Other Operators

Chapter Eight concentrated on the many new 'low-cost' operations that have been in the forefront of John Lennon Airport's tremendous expansion over the last ten years. This chapter deals with the other passenger, freight and mail services, and the 'general aviation' companies.

Prior to the arrival of easyJet, the bread-and-butter passenger services available from the airport were the scheduled Irish Sea routes to Belfast, Dublin and the Isle of Man, together with Inclusive Tour flights. The existing scheduled services flown by British Airways Regional to Belfast eventually succumbed to competition from easyJet and were withdrawn in May 2001. The services to Dublin, meanwhile, had been Ryanair's original operation into Liverpool, started in 1988 in competition with the long-standing Aer Lingus flights. Aer Lingus had withdrawn from the route in 1990 following Irish Government political directives to strengthen Ryanair's operations. This involved withdrawing Aer Lingus's traffic rights for a three-year period. Eventually, Aer Lingus did return to the Liverpool–Dublin route on 31 October 2004 with a daily operation. The Aer Lingus service was withdrawn once more on 25 June 2006, despite carrying many thousands of passengers during its new period of operation.

The Isle of Man route has been subject to a great deal of 'chopping and changing' with scheduled flights by a number of operators. For many years the service had been operated very successfully by Manx Airlines, but in February 2002 it was announced that this Isle of Man-based airline would lose its identity and become merged into the operations of British Airways, which had owned the company for some years. This move initiated interests in the Isle of Man to set up a locally based airline, EuroManx Airways, which commenced Liverpool–Isle of Man scheduled services on 2 December 2002. This service flew in competition with British Airways Regional until the latter company withdrew in March 2004. EuroManx initially operated as a booking agency, with its services being flown by other operators (Rossair and then Denim Airways) but EuroManx now has a number of its own DHC-8 aircraft, and hires in other larger aircraft under long-term contract.

Because the Isle of Man Government encourages competition on air routes to the island, two other airlines have flown in competition with EuroManx in recent years. There was also a brief operation by the Liverpool-based company, Keenair, prior to EuroManx starting its services. The first period of competition started soon after British

Airways withdrew from the route, when Emerald Airways ('Flyjem') re-started passenger flights to the island on 10 May 2004. These flights continued until 13 June 2005, when an agreement with EuroManx came into effect, whereby Emerald withdrew from the route, but its aircraft were used to fly the majority of EuroManx Liverpool-Ronaldsway services. This arrangement continued until Emerald Airways' Air Operator's Certificate was suspended by the Civil Aviation Authority on 4 May 2006.

After Emerald had withdrawn its own passenger flights to the island in June 2005, the Irish carrier Aer Arran announced that it too would seek to operate in competition with EuroManx. Its Liverpool services started on 3 October 2005, but were withdrawn on 18 June 2006. With the Emerald ATP aircraft no longer available to fly for EuroManx, an agreement had been reached for the Aer Arran ATR-42 aircraft used on the Liverpool-Isle of Man route to now fly for EuroManx in place of Emerald, and this arrangement continues as this book goes to press. Most of the services are thus flown by the larger Aer Arran aircraft, with supplementary flights by EuroManx's own 'Dash-8s'.

Other than the Irish Sea routes, the main 'traditional' air service from Liverpool has been that to London. Such a service was flown from 1934 to 1939, 1944 to 1948 and 1955 to 1992, but only intermittently since then. The Belgian operator, VLM, flew the route to London City Airport during 1994, but withdrew after eleven months. VLM returned in 2004 (after a campaign led by the *Liverpool Daily Post* and the Merseyside Chamber of Commerce), with five return flights per day to London City, but this route was suspended again on 29 June 2007 due to poor traffic figures, largely arising (in the author's opinion) from targeted rail competition. The VLM service was a good product, but perhaps could have been better publicised, the 'VLM' name not being a very well-known 'brand'. For point-to-point traffic to London, the City Airport is good, but it is poor for onward flight connections. The main problem is that it is very difficult to obtain access to Heathrow – the best point for onward connections – because the cost of obtaining 'slots' for flights at the desired peak times is horrendous (quite literally costing millions of pounds to the flight operator). A successful operation requires both the point-to-point (Liverpool–London) traffic and onward traffic with journeys booked to other places by connecting flights from whatever London terminal the flight uses. The likelihood of the necessary 'slots' becoming available is very low unless operators are directed by some legally enforceable requirement to provide connecting services from domestic points. Even existing domestic air services from other UK regional airports are coming under threat of suspension because of the physical limits on the number of possible flights when set against the costs of acquiring 'slots' and the profits to be made by airlines using their allocation of slots for non-domestic flights (this being the reason for British Midland having withdrawn their Liverpool–Heathrow service in 1992).

As for other domestic air services, the main hope for the re-introduction of a network of such routes appeared, fairly briefly, in 2005. FlyBe is another operator that claims to be a low-cost airline, although it is still 'in transition', and its low-cost credentials seem to have been confused at times by ambitions in other directions. On 11 October 2004 it announced that in early 2005 it would start services from Liverpool to Belfast City, Edinburgh, Exeter, Glasgow, Jersey and Southampton, commencing with Belfast on 10 February. However, its operations were at best half-hearted and difficult to comprehend. It seems that the airline was really trying to establish itself at Manchester in preference to Liverpool, and perhaps was trying to 'prove' to itself that flights from Liverpool were not viable. For example, flights to Glasgow were started, and then abandoned only a few weeks later after the airline claimed that there was insufficient 'business' traffic. This would not have come as a surprise to those who could have observed that part of the period of full twice-daily operation was during the 'Glasgow Fairs' weeks, when many businesses in Glasgow are shut down. The Belfast operation was sustained at decreasing frequency for over twelve months, and the daily Southampton flights were flown for seventeen months. The weekend (summer only) Jersey operation continued until the end of the 2007 season, and presumably may continue in future years. However, this whole sorry affair (so far as Liverpool is concerned) must be seen against the background that FlyBe was probably even at that time negotiating to take over the remaining British Airways 'non-trunk' internal services, which finally came to fruition during early 2007. Nevertheless, FlyBe have announced that Liverpool–Isle of Man services will commence in March 2008, in competition with EuroManx.

FlyBe services

Destination	Start Date	Frequency	Suspension Date
Belfast City	10.2.05	Initially Five daily	24.3.07
Jersey	7.5.05	One weekly	(Summer only)
Southampton	12.5.05	Daily	2.9.07
Edinburgh	27.3.05	Daily	30.10.05
Glasgow	28.3.05	Twice daily	7.8.05
Exeter	16.6.05	Daily	13.2.06
Isle of Man	30.3.08	Three daily	

Air Wales

Before FlyBe appeared on the scene, the Welsh-based carrier Air Wales commenced services between Cardiff and Newcastle, flying via Liverpool in both directions. This service was announced at short notice and started on 8 December 2003; however, it suffered various operational problems and ceased on 18 January 2004. Air Wales's flights started again on the routing Cardiff–Liverpool–Aberdeen on 1 December 2004 but were withdrawn on 11 November 2005. This operator's services were dogged by frequent timetable changes, never a recipe for encouraging or maintaining custom, and it came as no surprise that the airline ceased operations not long after its Liverpool services were withdrawn.

Jet Magic

Jet Magic was an airline started optimistically by Irish entrepreneurs in Cork, and commenced services between Cork and Liverpool on 15 September 2003. The airline flew ERJ-145 jets on its services, an expensive hobby for a 'new start-up' operator, but many of its services based on Cork failed to be profitable, and the airline collapsed into bankruptcy on 28 January 2004.

Aer Arran

As mentioned above, Aer Arran operated Liverpool–Isle of Man scheduled services, but earlier they had also flown a service between Liverpool and Knock in western Ireland. This relied on the airline using an ATR-42 aircraft that was based at Knock to operate subsidised 'Public Service Obligation' (PSO) flights between Knock and Dublin, with the Liverpool flights being scheduled in between the morning and evening PSO flights. The Liverpool service commenced on 21 June 2004 but was withdrawn on 21 July 2005 on the day that Aer Arran's PSO contract ceased (to be taken over by a different airline) and it was unable to justify continuing to base an aircraft at Knock. On 6 April 2006, Aer Arran also started a summer-only service with four return flights per week between Liverpool and Galway, but it was withdrawn on 1 October 2006.

Air Malta

The Maltese national airline, Air Malta, commenced a twice-weekly service with Airbus A320 aircraft between Liverpool and Malta on 5 May 2007. Although at one point the flights were due to continue during the winter season, the flights ceased on 2 September 2007. However, the service will resume for the 2008 summer season. It is believed that the service was an attempt by Air Malta to pre-empt 'low-cost' services being flown between John Lennon Airport and Malta by Ryanair or easyJet, but it is supposed that the Air Malta flights were not very well supported. It remains to be seen whether one of the 'lo-cos' will start flights to Malta, but both the prospective operators have in the past held discussions with the Maltese government regarding services from the UK.

Inclusive tour flights have been part of the 'bread-and-butter' of John Lennon Airport for many years, although, before something of a resurgence in the 1990s, the number of flights and destinations were relatively insignificant when compared to those from many other UK regional airports. The coming of the Direct Holidays brand in 1995 changed all that, and both Direct Holidays (later taken over by MyTravel) and their competitors (mainly the Thompson group, now TUI) based aircraft at John Lennon during the summer seasons. The MyTravel Group used their own aircraft in some years and in others the based aircraft was an Airbus A320 chartered from Monarch Airlines. The Thompson aircraft was usually a Boeing 757, with a larger Boeing 767 brought in for traffic peaks. However, the total Inclusive Tour traffic from the UK is in decline, largely because of the growth of the low-cost operators and increasing use of the internet which enables individuals to make their own holiday arrangements. This is leading to a situation where Liverpool will no longer have dedicated aircraft based locally to perform the majority of the tour flights sold from IT operators' brochures. Some flights have always been flown as (so-called) 'W' operations – that is the aircraft that arrive from the overseas destinations with a passenger load and pick up an outward load at Liverpool. The aircraft might be based at the overseas destination of the flights, but quite possibly somewhere else entirely. Inclusive Tour flights organised by the major tour operators (such as TUI, MyTravel, First Choice and so on) and specialist ones concentrating on particular countries (like Balkan Holidays) may well continue to be flown from Liverpool for some time to come, but the trend is in decline.

Freight services

Once, annual totals of freight and mail handled by Liverpool Airport were much higher than they are now. This was partly because a great deal of the traffic consisted of newspapers printed in the north-west of England, and flown to Dublin, Belfast and the Isle of Man. Over recent years this traffic has disappeared, because printing is now done on a more 'local' basis, with the content distributed electronically to the print works. Other cargo traffic over the Irish Sea routes was often carried in the holds of the Liverpool-based passenger aircraft, and by the same aircraft flying in cargo configuration during the night. The traffic patterns have changed, with much freight now carried by parcel carriers (the likes of TNT and DHL) who own or charter aircraft to move freight between their depots. The main freight carrier at Liverpool at present is TNT, who started to fly from Liverpool to Cologne in 1988, later transferring to a new central depot in Liege. These regular flights operate over weekday nights, sometimes carrying traffic only between Liverpool and Liege, and sometimes combined with other routes (e.g. Dublin–Liverpool–Liege), dependent on the loads and the types of aircraft available. Most of TNT's Liverpool flights are by TNT's own BAe 146 freighters, or by Lockheed Electras chartered from Atlantic Airlines. It seems likely the 'classic' turboprop Electras will eventually be replaced by the ubiquitous Boeing 737s, but as this is written the Electras are still seen each week. Occasionally, TNT's large Russian-built Tupolev Tu-204s have been used.

For many years, between 1993 and 2006, many freight flights over Irish Sea routes were flown by the Liverpool-based operator Emerald Airways on behalf of parcel services, such as Lynx or DHL. However, on 4 May 2006, the Civil Aviation Authority suspended Emerald Airways' Air Operators Certificate (AOC) because of organisational problems that infringed conditions of the certificate. This led to the collapse of the airline and the suspension of its freight operations, based in the UK and Europe. The freight services flown from Liverpool were then consolidated with other operations, or transferred to surface shipment, and have not so far resulted in replacement freight flights.

A major operation flown from Liverpool since July 1979 was the network of mail flights (the 'spokes from Speke') based on a postal sorting office at the airport, where

Keenair have always used Piper products as the major part of their Liverpool Flying School training fleet, the present examples being Piper Tomahawks, such as G-LFSN seen here in September 2007. (Adrian Thompson)

Ravenair, the more recently arrived General Aviation organisation at Liverpool, also use Piper Tomahawks for training, but also have several twin-engined types for charter work. This example is G-RVRO. (Adrian Thompson)

Opposite: Helicentre is the Liverpool-based helicopter training and charter company, which also has a branch in Spain. The Robinson R22 is their main training type. This example, G-CBXK, has floats, but these helicopters usually fly with a skid-type undercarriage. (Adrian Thompson)

nightly flights arrived from points all over the UK, and their contents re-distributed to depart to their destinations on the outgoing flights. Typically, these flights arrived from and departed to Belfast, Glasgow, Edinburgh, Gatwick, Bristol and elsewhere. Eventually an alternative network started, based at Nottingham–East Midlands Airport, and when the Post Office was under pressure to rationalise these services, it was announced that the flights would fly only from East Midlands with effect from the end of 2003. After negotiation, some of the Liverpool flights were then reprieved, with a new network operating from 12 January 2004. However, after further changes in Post Office operations, which now place much less reliance on moving mail by air, the final dedicated mail flights from Liverpool were made early in October 2006. The 'lo-co' airlines do not carry freight or mail in their holds, since this would frustrate the quick turn-arounds essential to the success of their business model, so the mail carryings from Liverpool are currently 'nil', and the freight figures rely on the TNT Liege flights, freight charter flights (mainly for the Jaguar and Vauxhall car companies), and a small-scale operation for DHL.

General Aviation

Before concluding this chapter, it is important to mention the general aviation activities at LJLA. As mentioned earlier in this book, the operations of Keenair and Ravenair continue to be important contributors to the general aviation scene at Liverpool, with both providing flight training and aircraft maintenance facilities. The Helicentre similarly provides training and support for people wishing to fly helicopters. The Ravenair Company provide handling services for private and executive aircraft visiting Liverpool, as well as providing support for the locally based Cessna Citation executive aircraft of AD Aviation. The number of based aircraft (including airliners and the fleets of the four operators mentioned in this chapter) is in the order of one hundred.

10

Airport Infrastructure and Master Plan

We now move on to consider the development of the airport infrastructure over the years since 2003, which has seen further expansion of the terminal building and development of facilities within it. The extensions include 'over-bridges' from the building to take passengers over the airside roads when boarding aircraft. The extension work has been aided by 'Objective 1' grant funding from the European Economic Development Fund.

In addition, a further six aircraft parking stands have been built to the east of the terminal building, and covered walkways built to serve these and some of the existing stands. A fleet of large Cobus passenger buses has been purchased to take passengers to and from the more remote aircraft parking stands. Work has recently started on a combined airport hotel and multi-storey car park, within the existing ground-level car park. The hotel will complement 'off-airport' facilities, such as the Enterprise Inn recently built close to the airport approach road, and the Marriott South Hotel developed from the original Speke Airport terminal building. Planning applications for more nearby hotels may be expected.

Although freight traffic has declined, for reasons discussed in Chapter Nine, a new freight-handling building has been built for lease to TNT and was opened in June 2006. This is to the east of the newest aircraft parking stands, between them and the general aviation area. To promote travel of potential airport passengers on public transport, as opposed to using their cars, Merseytravel has developed the Liverpool South Parkway transport hub, which replaces railway stations on two railway lines (Merseyrail, and the West Coast main line) serving the south of Liverpool city and combines the new single station with a bus station that provides services to the airport and other parts of the city. This enables rail passengers to reach the airport from South Parkway in about ten minutes. Liverpool South Parkway received planning permission on 25 June and central government approval on 18 December 2003, and was opened on 11 June 2006.

The technical facilities have also developed, with a new Raytheon Systems ASR-10SS Mark 2 Air Traffic Control surveillance radar being installed during 2006, in place of the earlier Marconi S511. The radar (unusually) is used for monitoring and controlling traffic at the Doncaster–Sheffield Airport, also owned by Peel Airports, as well as Liverpool's traffic. During night closures in the 2006–07 winter season, the existing 09/27 'new' runway, originally opened in 1966, was effectively rebuilt. The top surface of the runway was replaced and the runway lighting upgraded to enable the airport to operate in weather conditions down to Category IIIB (that is, horizontal visibility of between 50 and 200m and vertical visibility of 50ft or less), subject to the aircraft being equipped and their crews cleared to make landing approaches in these conditions. Prior to these changes, which are still being finalised as this is written, approaches to Liverpool John Lennon in bad visibility could only be made in 'Category II' conditions, with horizontal visibility above 350m. The Instrument Landing System on Runway 27 already met the accuracy requirements for Category IIIB approval, but the approach runway and taxiway lights needed to be enhanced in order to match the performance of the ILS.

Master Plan

In accordance with central government requirements, all regional airports have been asked to prepare Master Plans, detailing their plans for development over the period to the year 2030. The draft Master Plan for Liverpool was issued for public consultation during 2006, and will be finalised in the light of comments from interested parties towards the end of 2007. Plans are just that; they may or may not come to pass, depending on events and changes in requirements. However, some general points can be made arising from study of the draft.

The main developments considered in the Master Plan include enhanced surface access to the airport from surrounding areas, although further extension of the

Draft Master Plan to 2015.

terminal facilities and a modest runway extension are also considered. Up to the year 2015, all the developments under consideration envisage expansion on the northern side of the existing runway, i.e. further development of the existing buildings, aircraft parking areas, car parks and landside roads. After 2015, it would become necessary to construct additional facilities on the south side of the runway in the area known as the Oglet, where the only existing building is the Air Traffic Control Tower (built in 2001), although a new fire station is planned to be constructed near the tower in the near-term. The other additional facilities would tend to be buildings for air freight and aircraft maintenance, which would have been 'squeezed out' of the areas on the north side.

The question of the runway extension may depend on the need to provide for aircraft taking off on long-range flights, carrying either passengers or freight. The plan provides for a runway extension to the east of 314m, together with 'starter strips' of 150m at each end of the runway. 'Starter strips' are narrow extensions that are only used for take-off (as the aircraft begins to accelerate to the runway proper) and are not declared to be part of the usable runway for landing. Allied to the possible extensions, the road under the approach at the eastern end (Dungeon Lane) would be closed. As well as accommodating the eastern starter strip, this would enable the approach lighting at that end of the runway to be incorporated within the airport boundary, which is becoming a requirement imposed on airports by regulatory authorities such as the Civil Aviation Authority. All of these changes will of course require planning permission and other approvals, which may be more difficult to achieve in these days of perceived concern about aviation's contribution to global warming.

11

Air Display Memories

Reprinted with permission from *Rapide*, the magazine for the north-west vintage aviation enthusiast.

The Great Liverpool Air Display, by Don Stephens

The May public holiday weekend in 1956 was very busy for aviation enthusiasts on Merseyside. Almost all went to the Armed Forces Day at Burtonwood near Warrington on Saturday 19th May with the Speke Pageant scheduled for Whit Monday, 21st May.

Most of us guessed that there would be practice flyovers or other activity on the intervening day, mostly at Speke. However, I went to Burtonwood first, thinking that I might see the F-86 Sabres of the 'Skyblazers' aerobatic team. It seemed reasonable since the official programme, that cost me one shilling (5p), said they were booked to perform at Speke. Instead, I saw the smart T-33s of the USAF's other display team, the 'Acrojets' who went on to display at Yeadon on the Monday.

Arriving at Speke, it was good to see a hive of activity. Readers must bear in mind that these were the gloomy days of the Airport's under-utilisation. Many a time I have pedalled to Speke only to see just a single aircraft in front of the terminal – usually it would be a BEA or Aer Lingus Dakota.

As we had surmised, this day was to be different. Four Canberras and eight Vampires did practice flights over the airfield. Meteor T.7 WF778 of 613 (City of Manchester) Squadron visited from Ringway in connection with the display.

The Deperdussin came up by road from Old Warden. The Spitfire flew in from Chilbolton. The diminutive SIPA S-200 Minijet landed and a Meteor and Venom arrived by road for the static display. They were some of the tasters for the excitement promised by the next day.

Although organized by SSAFA (Soldiers, Sailors and Airmens Families Association) in the hope of swelling its funds, the *Liverpool Daily Post* and Liverpool Echo newspapers sponsored the proceedings. In those days The Echo sold far more widely than today, presumably because most folk still lacked television sets.

Looking at the yellowing pages of the Liverpool newspapers fifty years later convinces me what a good job they did in promoting 'the first Speke air display since the war'.

I arrived early. In perfect weather I joined the crowds walking down the road past the Bryant and May match factory. As a result, I entered 'White' sector from Speke Road. My first target was the static display near No.2 Hangar, dominated by Beverley XB283 of 47 Squadron. In addition the RAF Publicity Unit at 71 MU Bicester had sent Meteor NF 11 WM185 and the first Venom FB1 to be built at Chester, 7137M (WE270).

As I write this I am glancing at a notebook bearing the title of Quarry Bank High School on the cover and containing the jottings of the day. I recall that the school had given it to me for a rather different purpose! Also, I have an article that I wrote shortly after the event, either for Air-Britain or Registration Research, which gives the structure of the flying display. Anybody who has an official programme should ignore the list of aircraft scheduled to fly. The fact is that the programme could not work out as planned. The events are in the wrong order and two advertised display items did not proceed at all.

The Blackburn B2, if it had come, would presumably have been G-AEBJ, then maintained at Brough by the manufacturing company. The loss of the Valiant from the programme was disappointing, but understandable. On 11th May, while serving at RAE Farnborough, Valiant WP202 had crashed at Brighton. The AOC in Chief of Bomber Command, Air Marshal Sir Harry Broadhurst, issued an order prohibiting the Valiant from flying from RAF Wyton in Cambridgeshire until the enquiries into the accident were complete.

Later I was to learn that the 1962 air display, held at the same time of year drew a crowd of about 30,000. It is not hard to imagine the crush in 1956, when at least 120,000 packed into the airfield. During the flying display, lasting from 2 pm to about 5 pm, there was not much chance of moving position. I selected my spot and basically stuck to it. Remember that the main runway, 08–26, was operational the whole day and it becomes obvious that the main throng was crammed into both the Speke Hall side down to the river and various parts of the Airport on or adjacent to the terminal.

Before I write about the flying display, here is a list of other aircraft reportedly seen on the airfield on 21st May: Spitfire PR.19 PS915, which did the Temperature & Humidity ('Thum') flight that day; Rapide GAFRK of Air Views; Auster J1NAlpha G-AJUL of Blackpool & Fylde Aero Club; Aiglet Trainer G-AMTC belonging to Airways Aero Associations: Ferranti's Autocar GAOBV; Martin Baker's Prince G-AMLY; Dakotas G-AGJZ and 'MJY (BEA); and 'MJU (Starways); Anson G-AIPA (R.J. Gates/Federated Fruit) and the cannibalized remains of another ex-RN Anson, N9828 (in the process of being reduced to spares for Federated Fruit); Heron 2E GAOGU of Cambrian Airways; Rapides G-ALEJ (Lancashire Aircraft Corp'n.) and G-AIBB (R.J. Gates-Federated Fruit); Auster 5 G-ANHO (belonging to racing driver Ron Flockhart) was seen near the clubhouse hangar); and Autocrat G-AGYP (another Ferranti owned aircraft). Other home-based aircraft and visitors are mentioned later. Alert readers will have already observed that the contents of No.1 Hangar are not mentioned, presumably they included some Sabres undergoing service work by Airwork. So far as I am aware no inquisitive observer saw into that hangar as it was in an area designated as a coach park. The map explains the layout better than words.

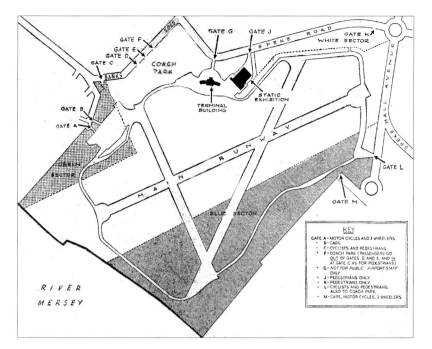

This plan, reproduced from the Air Display Programme, amplifies the description of the airfield layout.

The display started at 2 pm. As a matter of record, aircraft operated in the direction of the 08 runway (i.e. from the River Mersey inland).

The vintage Deperdussin Monoplane (nowadays G-AANH) stuttered across the airfield at what I thought was little more than about twenty feet up. Jeffrey Quill expertly handled the wing warping to control this relic from 1910. The Deperdussin had been used at Hendon until the First World War. The Shuttleworth Collection acquired it from a private owner in 1935. It had been maintained so well that it was a treat to see it some years later on in the film 'Those Magnificent Men in Their Flying Machines'.

While the Deperdussin made its demonstration flight, the Westland Dragonfly HR.3 helicopter from RNAS Anthorn had started up. This was WP494 (code '900/ AH'), one of the last twelve of the type ordered for the Royal Navy.

Next came the SIPA S-200 Minijet F-BGVN (constructor's number 04), one of nine to be built. Alan Hisler, who was an experienced aerobatic pilot, caught everybody's attention with a sparkling performance. He flew inverted in front of us, climbed for height, dived and zoomed at high speed across the airfield. In retrospect I believe it looked faster than it was because the aircraft was so tiny ('like a little Vampire', as a friend commented).
Later in the day, Hisler took off to repeat his efforts at Yeadon. This splendid little aeroplane designed by Yves Gardan and built in 1952 was powered by a single Turbomeca Palas developing 350 pounds of thrust. Essentially, the Minijet was a rich man's toy. Look on to the Internet and you will see one of two survivors up for sale for 200,000 US dollars.

At 2.30 pm, eight Vampires from 613 Squadron, stationed at Ringway, flew over. The photograph in the programme shows four aircraft leading another four.

The Supermarine Spitfire V (AB910) flown by Jeffrey Quill in the display. (Photograph by Don Stephens)

As a result, the early MGAE (Merseyside Group of Aviation Enthusiasts) members, scattered in the crowd, all focused their binoculars on the leading four aircraft, intent on jotting down serial numbers.

Every witness I have consulted has the serials of the leading four Vampires but nobody appears to have any record of the following four. The leaders were VZ118, VZ264, WA107 - all FB.5s - and WR257, an FB.9. If only they had done another pass we might have a complete record! Little did the Auxiliaries know that a Tory government would abolish them in the year following. They were near their literal end.

The 613 Squadron display was followed by Leo Valentin's ('The Birdman') first appearance, a delayed parachute drop from a Rapide.

A contrast came as Tiger Moth G-AGYU of Marshall Flying Services towed a red Slingsby Sky sailplane. This was piloted by Gerard Smith, CFI of the Derby and Lancs Gliding Club, who, after some carefully performed aerobatics, put the glider down next to its trailer. A reliable source tells me that BGA 686 is still active over fifty years later. It is now called 'Kinder Scout II' and based at Camphill, Great Hucklow in Derbyshire.

At 2.50 pm, five Supermarine Attacker FB2s from 1831 RNVR Squadron, from RNAS Stretton, made their debut. The five aircraft were: WZ283 (810/ST), WK341 (811/ST), WK321 (813/ST), WP276 (814/ST) and WZ294 (816/ST). Four of the Attackers proceeded to show what agile aeroplanes they were. My little notebook tells me that while these four entertained the crowd, the fifth appeared to have gone. Suddenly, 810/ST gave the crowd a shock by flying in low, fast and deliberately unannounced, trailing red smoke.

Then came my favourite moment of the day: Spitfire Vb AB910 was demonstrated to perfection by a test pilot who had flown the first Spitfire in the 1930s, Jeffrey Quill.

The climbing rolls and all-round agility of the Spitfire allied to that distinctive Merlin sound had me entranced. At the time I did not know that this Spitfire had had a fine front-line career in the war, nor that it was the Spitfire that took off from Hibaldstow in 1945 with LACW Margaret Horton, a WAAF ground crew fitter, sitting on the tail. Pilot, plane and WAAF were fortunate to live through the experience.

More impressive is the fact that AB910 destroyed a Do 217 during the Dieppe Raid and flew patrols over the Normandy invasion beaches on 'the longest day'.

At 3.05 pm the 'Skyblazers' Sabres arrived to start their close formation routine. It was a coveted distinction to be in the team of pilots. On the afternoon of the Pageant they were in F-86Fs. Our MGAE witnesses recorded their serial numbers as 31201 (FU 201), 31186 (FU186), 31192 (FU192) and 31219 (FU219). They came from 48th Fighter/Bomber Wing based at Chaumont Air Base in France. The final "bomb burst" with smoke ended a good, well-rehearsed display.

The next item was a so-called 'parachute race' between two men. The official programme describes this as a 'novel event, which has not been staged before in this country'. Trapped in the crowd, I watched, but thought it was tame compared with the aircraft.

Then four Canberra T.4s flew past in a stately manner. They were: WE190, WJ863, WN467 and WT490. The practice run on the day before included WJ 877 in place of WE190. The voice on the loud speaker said they were from 10 Squadron, but that was incorrect. WE190 and WT490 were officially with Wyton Station Flight, WJ863 with Cottesmore Station Flight and WN467 with Honington Station Flight. It is likely that at this date these 'Station Flight' aircraft were really from 231 OCU, Bassingbourn. Certainly instructors from the OCU would have flown them.

Immediately following came Sea Hawks from 767 Squadron stationed at RNAS Ford. They were: WM920 (709/FD), WM925(710/FD), WF275 (711/FD) and WM908 (712/FD). 767 Squadron was a Fighter Pilot Pool Squadron undertaking general training.

Judging by the quality of the flying, the pilots might well have been instructors.

At this point the Beverley made a demonstration flight, much to the pleasure of some of us. Immediately following came four Meteor F.8s of 74 Squadron, Horsham St. Faith. They were: WA824, WF712, WK816 and (probably) WA879. The MGAE contingent, even though split up, found it tricky to note their serials and be unanimous about their single-letter codes.

As they completed their demonstration, Starways Dakota G-AMPY, with port-side freight doors removed, taxied out for takeoff. The bright orange wings of Leo Valentin, 'The Birdman', could be seen forward of the door space.

While Captain George Leigh climbed to 9,000 feet, a BEA Pionair-class Dakota landed and the Airwork Viking G-AKTU took off. Also, the Taylorcraft Plus D and Austers went up to position themselves for the last item in the programme.

At the time, we all agreed, it seemed to take a very long while for 'MPY to climb into position. My notes say that the Dakota took off at 4 pm. We know that Valentin jumped at 4.23 pm. He intended to use his wings to glide for some time, before parachuting down to earth. Most of the crowd were looking at the spot on the grass as indicated by the commentator. Through my new binoculars, I watched Valentin fall vertically down until he disappeared from sight behind No.2 Hangar. His vertical drop made me guess the worst. The crowd was not told of the fatal accident, but a doctor was called for. The Dragonfly helicopter flew off in the direction of the accident. I did not know until later that Valentin had recently written a book about being a 'Birdman', nor that he was a married man of thirty-seven with a daughter aged thirteen. His next stop was Widnes mortuary. It was a great tragedy.

The commentator for the day, who handled the event so expertly, was Kenneth Wolstenholme. He had been a much decorated bomber pilot who had flown over 100 operations. Later he would add to his fame by commenting on England's World Cup football win in 1966.

The final two items took place as scheduled. Forty-six year old Dragoljub Aleksic, first with one foot on the bottom rung and his head pointing down towards the earth 150 feet below him. Then he swung his body and hung below the rope ladder, sustained only by his bite on the bottom rung. It was a good thing that the Tiger Moth he used (G-AOHC) flew along sedately. Even with his own pilot (Miroslav Stoka) at the controls, it was a dangerous stunt that could easily have led to fatality number two. Aleksic waved a Yugoslav flag and then a British one. Really, he was not an airman at all, just a professional acrobat.

Finally, the three aircraft of the Merseyside and North Wales Flying Club (G-AHAK, IPH and JAE), smart in their red and white livery, flew past in farewell salute to the crowd.

It was over. That night as I pondered what I had seen at the Pageant, I mentally voted the Spitfire as my favourite display item. I must have been to scores of air displays before and since, but never one like this. If you were there, have you ever been to anything quite like it? Spitfire AB910, still extant with the Battle of Britain Memorial Flight, testifies that the type has remained a symbol of all that is fine in life at a time of great need.

The Spitfire Vb G-AISU (AB910) was built at Castle Bromwich in 1941. It was allocated to No.222 (Natal) Squadron at North Weald on 22nd August 1941, then re-allocated to No.130 Squadron with whom it flew several convoy patrols and also daylight escort patrols to the bombing raids against the German battle cruisers Scharnhorst and Gneisenau during their 'Channel dash'. In June 1942, AB910 was delivered to No.133 (Eagle) Squadron, at Biggin Hill. The aircraft flew 29 operational missions with this unit, including four sorties on 19th August 1942 during the fierce aerial battles in support of the Dieppe Raid, her pilots being credited with one Dornier Do 217 destroyed and one damaged during these combats. AB910 continued to fly operationally up to July 1944, serving with No.242 (Canadian) and Nos.416 and 402 (RCAF) Squadrons. With 402 Squadron she flew numerous cover patrols over the Normandy invasion beach-heads on D-Day itself (6th June 1944) and on subsequent days. In addition to these operational assignments, AB910 was held on charge by various maintenance units and, after mid-July 1944, she was relegated to support duties with No.53 OTU at Hibaldstow and then with No.527 Squadron (a radar calibration unit).

Later, AB910 was acquired by Group Captain (later Air Commodore) Allen Henry Wheeler, formerly Commanding Officer Experimental Flying at RAE Farnborough (in 1942-1943 at least) and later Commandant of the A&AEE Boscombe Down). He owned it from 25th October 1946, until 6th August 1955 and planned on using the aircraft for air-racing. Wheeler was also a leading figure in the Shuttleworth Trust and owned another Spitfire, a Westland-built Mk 1a, AR213/G-AIST, although the latter did very little, or perhaps no, flying - it was stored dismantled at Old Warden for many years.

G-AISU did make appearances at Old Warden, but the airfield was then too small for the Spitfire to fly from. By the time of the 1956 Display at Speke, AB910 was owned by Vickers-Armstrongs (Aircraft) Ltd and Jeffrey Quill usually flew it for them. Vickers presented AB910 to the Battle of Britain Flight in 1965 and it flies with that unit today.

A list of other air displays at Liverpool is shown below:

11.6.32	Cobham's flying circus
1.7.33	Official opening air display
25.5.35	'Empire Air Day' with Cobham's Air Circus
28.5.38	'Empire Air Day' with extensive RAF participation
26.5.62	'At Home'
1.6.63	'At Home'
1.5.71	'Wings over Merseyside'
29.4.72	'Wings over Merseyside'
12.5.73	'Wings over Merseyside'
18.9.77	'Silver Jubilee Air Rally'
8.7.78	'Air Rally'
21.6.81	'Liverpool Air Show'
27.6.82	'Liverpool Air Show'
18 & 19.8.84	'Air & Transport Extravaganza'

In addition to those listed, there was a visit by 'The Crimson Fleet', a rival to Alan Cobham's Air Circus, during 1932 and one by another rival, the British Hospitals' Air Pageant on 7th August 1933. A further visit was made to 'Liverpool' by the Cobham Circus on 21st July 1934.

Finally, there was a display held on 29th July 1939, when the Lord Mayor and Corporation of Liverpool carried out a Review of the Speke-based No.611 (West Lancashire) Squadron of the Auxiliary Air Force. This last was covered in an issue of 'Pictures from the Post' (published by the *Liverpool Daily Post*), but the writer has been unable to obtain a copy. Any offers?

The interesting adjacent photograph, taken during the Empire Air Display on 28 May 1938, shows the crowd in front of the 'Station Building' (Terminal Building), which was still under construction around the Control Tower at the time and was only completed towards the end of the year.

Appendices

Appendix 1: The 1938 Terminal Building

The 1938 station building was influenced by the building at Hamburg-Fuhlsbuttel Airport in Germany, which had (among others) been inspected by a delegation from Liverpool in 1935. The Liverpool building was, however, built to a very high standard to an original design by the Liverpool City Engineers' Department. It was the pre-eminent municipal airport building in Great Britain prior to the Second World War, only that at Birmingham's Elmdon Airport coming anywhere near to rivalling it.

The building was first used in 1938, but there was never an official 'opening ceremony'; one was being considered in 1939 as some ancillary works on surrounding roadways came to an end, but the onset of the Second World War intervened, with part of the building being prepared for use as an RAF training school in the weeks before the outbreak of war. The building was designed to handle traffic arriving in small biplanes (such as the DH Rapide), but when it fell out of use in 1986 it had handled passengers from Boeing 747 jumbo jets, having suffered very few internal alterations in the meantime. The building became 'listed' as a structure of historic importance, and under the care of the Speke Garston Development Company and Neptune Developments it now has been sensitively restored to its former glory. The adjacent hangars have similarly been preserved as an 'ensemble' to show the setting of the group of former airport buildings and aircraft parking area in an imaginative way.

Projects of the Speke Garston Development Company, and its successor the Liverpool Land Development Company, in conjunction with developers, Neptune Developments:

Marriott Hotel (former terminal building) opened 15 May 2001 (investment £12 million).
David Lloyd Leisure Centre (former No.1 Hangar) opened in January 2000 (investment £10 million).
Littlewoods Shop Direct Group Headquarters 'Skyways House' (former No.2 Hangar) refurbishment completed in stages from 2001-2006 (investment £31 million, including Littlewoods' fitting-out).

Right and below:
The restored
'Hangar No.2', now
'Skyways House'
for the Littlewoods

Appendix 2: Aircraft produced by Rootes Securities Ltd

Contract 551920/36 for 600 Bristol Blenheim (produced as 250 Mk I and 350 Mk IV)

Mark I

L8362 to L8407	(46)	L8433 to L8482	(50)	L8500 to L8549	(50)
L8597 to L8632	(36)	L8652 to L8701	(50)	L8714 to L8731	(18)

Mark IV

L8732 to L8761	(30)	L8776 to L8800	(25)	L8827 to L8876	(50)
L9020 to L9044	(25)	L9170 to L9218	(49)	L9237 to L9273	(37)
L9294 to L9342	(49)	L9375 to L9422	(48)	L9446 to L9482	(37)

Contract B.982940/39 for 420 Short S.29 Stirling Mk I, Rootes advised 8 March 1939

Although an instruction to proceed was issued for this contract, enabling Rootes to spend money on tooling, materials and other preparatory work, the prospective contract was cancelled on 20

May 1940. No serial numbers were allotted to the Stirlings, although these were usually given at the instruction to proceed stage. Serial numbers beginning with the letter P would have been current at the date of the ITP.

Contract B.1485/39/C.36(a), initially for 250 Blenheim IV aircraft

Rootes advised 13 April 1939

R3590 to R3639	(50)	R3660 to R3709	(50)	R3730 to R3779	(50)
R3800 to R3849	(50)	R3870 to R3919	(50)		

400 additional Mk IV, Rootes advised 27.09.39

T1793 to T1832	(40)	T1848 to T1897	(50)	T1921 to T1960	(40)
T1985 to T2004	(20)	T2031 to T2080	(50)	T2112 to T2141	(30)
T2161 to T2190	(30)	T2216 to T2255	(40)	T2273 to T2292	(20)
T2318 to T2357	(40)	T2381 to T2400	(20)	T2425 to T2444	(20)

800 additional Mk IV, Rootes advised 22.12.39

V5370 to V5399	(30)	V5420 to V5469	(50)	V5490 to V5539	(50)
V5560 to V5599	(40)	V5620 to V5659	(40)	V5680 to V5699	(20)
V5720 to V5769	(50)	V5790 to V5829	(40)	V5850 to V5899	(50)
V5920 to V5969	(50)	V5990 to V6039	(50)	V6060 to V6099	(40)
V6120 to V6149	(30)	V6170 to V6199	(30)	V6220 to V6269	(50)
V6290 to V6339	(50)	V6420 to V6469	(50)	V6490 to V6529	(40)

600 additional Mark IV, Rootes advised June 1940

Z7271 to Z7320	(50)	Z7340 to Z7374	(35)	Z7406 to Z7455	(50)
Z7483 to Z7522	(40)	Z7577 to Z7596	(20)	Z7610 to Z7654	(45)
Z7678 to Z7712	(35)	Z7754 to Z7803	(50)	Z7841 to Z7860	(20)
Z7879 to Z7928	(50)	Z7958 to Z7992	(35)		

(430 built, other aircraft cancelled)

A small number of the aircraft from this last batch, although built at Speke, were assembled and test-flown at RAF Shawbury or at Meir Airport, Stoke-on-Trent, adjacent to the Blythe Bridge factory, as a build-up to production at Blythe Bridge.

780 additional aircraft were built as Mk V, mostly at Blythe Bridge, but fifty of them were built at Speke in parallel with early production at Blythe Bridge. Rootes were advised 21 August 1940 and serial numbers commenced AZ861 (built at Blythe Bridge). The fifty Speke aircraft included AZ927, AZ928, AZ936, AZ937, AZ939, AZ940, AZ941, AZ945, AZ946, AZ948, AZ950, AZ951, AZ953, AZ954, AZ955, AZ958, AZ959, AZ960, AZ962, AZ964, AZ965 and AZ986. A further twenty-eight with earlier AZ numbers have not been specifically identified.

Contract B.124276/40 for two prototype Bristol Bisley (Blenheim Mk V)

The order for the aircraft initially serialled AA276 & AA279 was cancelled and then reinstated with the aircraft becoming DJ702 and DJ707. These were built at Speke and flew after the Bristol-built prototypes, but before the Speke-built production aircraft.

Contracts/Aircraft/637/C.4(c) for 150 Handley Page Halifax B Mk II (*c*.31 January 1941)

DG219 to DG230   (12 completed as Mk II. Remainder of contract built as Mk V)
DG231 to DG253   (23)   DG270 to DG317 (48)   DG338 to DG363   (26)
DG384 to DG424   (41)

100 additional B Mk II, changed to Mk V before delivery, ordered 04.08.41
EB127 to EB160   (34)   EB178 to EB220   (43)   EB239 to EB258   (29)
EB274 to EB276   (3)

480 additional B Mk V, ordered 29.03.42
LK890 to LK932   (43)   LK945 to LK976   (32)   LK988 to LK999   (12)
LL112 to LL153   (42)   LL167 to LL198   (32)   LL213 to LL258   (46)
LL270 to LL312   (43)   LL325 to LL367   (43)   LL380 to LL423   (44)
LL437 to LL469   (33)   LL481 to LL521   (41)   LL534 to LL542   (9)
(all above built as Mk V)
LL543 to LL559   (17)   LL573 to LL615   (43)
(these last 60 aircraft completed as Mk III)

360 additional B Mk III, ordered 28.09.42
MZ945 to MZ989   (45)   NA102 to NA150   (49)   NA162 to NA205   (44)
NA218 to NA263   (46)   NA275 to NA309   (35)
(219 built as B Mk III)
NA310 to NA320   (11)   NA336 to NA380   (45)   NA392 to NA431   (40)
NA444 to NA468   (25)
(121 built as A Mk VII airborne forces transports)
(NA469 to NA488 were cancelled, leaving 340 built from this addition to the contract)

In addition to the twenty cancelled aircraft given above, a further 600 aircraft with numbers between PX534 and PX909 and between SV344 and SV736 were cancelled with the approach of the end of the Second World War. Other Rootes Securities Ltd contracts at Speke covered the production of Blenheim and Halifax spare parts, the recovery of usable parts from crashed Blenheims, the modification of Blenheims built by Rootes, A.V. Roe and other manufacturers to have tropical equipment fitted, and the modification of bomber Halifaxes received from RAF units to take on other roles, such as anti-submarine warfare or meteorological reconnaissance. In addition, the Blythe Bridge factory built Bristol Beaufighters, assembled and modified North American Harvards and Mustangs for the RAF, and carried out modifications to USAAF P-47 Thunderbolts and RAF Liberator bombers, but (despite reports to the contrary) none of this work was done at the Speke factory. The number of aircraft built by the Speke factory totalled 3,602.

The factory was handed over to the Dunlop Rubber Co. Ltd for post-war use and provided employment for Liverpool people for many years. The flight shed became a production line for conveyor belts, while the main factory made new and remoulded tyres, golf balls and other rubber products. Eventually the fortunes of the Dunlop company declined and the factory closed. It was demolished in September 1987.

Newly discovered views of aircraft production at the Rootes' factory. Here Bristol Blenheims are outside the Flight Shed, and censor's marks show where views of Speke Church should be deleted.

More than twenty Halifaxes dispersed around the factory and on the airfield, in around 1943. In the distance are rows of Vultee Vengeances dive-bombers after shipment from the USA. (Palatine Studios 3000-727 via The Handley Page Association)

The sole remaining relic of the aircraft factory's production is the Halifax VII NA337, one of the airborne forces transports from the last Rootes order. This was shot down in Norway in 1945, but it landed on a frozen lake and sank through the ice. The aircraft was recovered in recent years and taken to Canada, where it has been restored in memory of the use of many Halifaxes by squadrons of the Royal Canadian Air Force based in Yorkshire during the Second World War. The aircraft is now on display at the RCAF Memorial Museum at Canadian Forces' Base, Trenton, Ontario.

Appendix 3: Service Units and their Aircraft

Royal Air Force First-Line Units

Squadron	Code letters	Aircraft type	Typical aircraft serial nos	From	To
No.236	FA-	Blenheim IF	K7140, K7143, L1301	North Coates 23.04.40	Filton 25.05.40
No.13	OO-	Lysander II	N1246, P9056, R2027	Hooton Park 16.06.40	Hooton Park 13.07.40

Squadron	Code letters	Aircraft type	Typical aircraft serial nos	From	To
No.312	DU-	Hurricane I	L1547, P3612, V6810	Duxford 26.09.40	Valley 03.03.41
No.229	RE-	Hurricane I	P3114, P3588, V7077	Wittering 22.12.40	(Middle East) 10.05.41
No.315	PK-	Hurricane I	P3026, R4122, V7187	Acklington 13.03.41	Northolt 16.07.41
No.303	RF-	Spitfire I	R6993, X4339, X4828	Northolt 17.07.41	Northolt 07.10.41
No.306	UZ-	Spitfire II	P8193	Northolt 07.10.41	Church Stanton 12.12.41
MSFU	KE-, LU-, NJ-	Sea Hurricane I	N2660, P3620, V7043	(Formed) 05.05.41	(Disbanded) 07.09.43

Royal Air Force Second-Line Units

Unit	Aircraft type and typical serial nos	From	To
No.8 Radio Maintenance Unit	Hornet Moth W9389	(Formed) 10.07.40	To No.8 RSS
No.8 Radio Servicing Section	Hornet Moth W5753 Blenheim I K7161, L1200	No.8 R.M.U. 01.10.40	To No.77 (S) Wing
No.77 (Signals) Wing Calibration Flight	Hornet Moth W5779 Blenheim IV R3615	From No.8 RSS 17.02.41	(Disbanded) 18.06.43
Station Flight Speke	Magister N3835 Tiger Moth N6465 Hurricane I P3485	(Formed) ...10.40	(Disbanded) ...11.43
Liverpool University Air Squadron	Tiger Moth L6933	(Formed) 04.01.41	Sealand ...01.46
No.116 Squadron (detachments)	Lysander III T1635, V9619 (Code II-)	(Formed) 31.03.41	Hucknall 30.04.41
		Hooton Park 11.06.42	Woodvale 15.11.42
No.9 Group Anti-Aircraft Co-operation Unit	Lysander II P1731 Blenheim IV Z5873	(Formed) 25.05.41	Wrexham 06.08.41
No.15 Group Communications Flight	Dominie P9589, Q.6 P5636, Oxford AS735 Proctor DX187	Hooton Park 15.12.42	(Disbanded) 01.08.45
No.186 Elementary Gliding School	Dagling Kirby Cadet I RA905	(Formed) ...06.44	Hooton Park ...03.47

Fleet Air Arm Units

Unit	Aircraft type and typical serial nos	From	To
No.776 Squadron	Roc L3171, Skua L3033 Chesapeake AL944, Hurricane P5206, Oxford HN126, Martinet PW958, Swordfish V4320, Blenheim I L6764, Seafire II NM973, Fulmar DR633, Defiant AA294, Dominie X7508, Sea Gladiator N2276	Lee-on-Solent 22.03.41	Woodvale 07.04.45
No.829 Squadron	Swordfish II	Lee-on-Solent 19.02.42	Macrihanish 25.02.42
No.849 Squadron	Avenger	HMS *Khedive* 17.11.43	Grimsetter 25.11.43
No.1832 Squadron	Wildcat V	Eglinton 20.09.43	Stretton 09.12.43
No.1834 Squadron	Corsair II	Maydown 19.11.43	Maydown 22.11.43
No.787Y Flight	Dominie, Seafire III	Burscough 12.11.44	Macrihanish 15.01.45
No.736B Flight	Seafire III	(Formed) 01.03.45	HMS *Colossus* 11.03.45
No.1820 Squadron	Helldiver	HMS *Arbiter* 24.07.44	Burscough 11.08.44

Appendix 4: Major Airline Users and Other Operators

Carrier	From	To
Aer Lingus Teoranta	14.09.1936	15.01.1990
BKS Air Transport	25.04.1960	31.03.1976
Blackpool & West Coast Air Services	03.07.1933	30.06.1946
British Airways	01.04.1976	28.10.1978
British Eagle International Airlines	01.01.1964	06.11.1968
British European Airways Corporation	01.02.1947	31.03.1963
British Midland Airways	29.10.1978	27.10.2001
Cambrian Airways	07.04.1951	31.03.1976
Dan-Air Services Ltd.	01.04.1960	Mar. 1975
easyJet	26.10.1997	current
Emerald Airways (Passenger operations)	29.04.1996	26.03.1999
(Freight operations, initially as Janes Aviation)	01.06.1993	current
Euromanx	02.12.2002	current
Federated Air Transport	02.12.1953	20.02.1961
Genair	03.08.1981	13.07.1984
Great Western and Southern Air Lines	01.05.1939	30.08.1939
Hillman's Airways	16.07.1934	30.09.1935
Isle of Man Air Services	27.09.1937	31.01.1947
KLM	01.06.1934	30.08.1939
Manx Airlines/BA CitiExpress	01.11.1982	28.03.2004

Carrier	From	To
Midland and Scottish Air Ferries	14.08.1933	14.07.1934
Northern & Scottish Airways	01.07.1936	20.05.1937
Railway Air Services	07.05.1934	31.01.1947
Ryanair	26.05.1988	current
Skytravel	20.06.1946	15.08.1947
Starways Ltd	May 1949	31.12.1963
Steiner's Air and Travel Services	06.11.1946	25.11.1947
TNT (initially as Air Foyle)	06.02.1988	current
United Airways	18.06.1935	01.10.1935
Vernair (General Aviation)	22.05.1967	07.03.1987
Liverpool and District Aero Club	01.04.1934	31.08.1939
Wright Aviation	21.04.1950	31.12.1953
Dragon Airways	10.09.1953	01.11.1955
Keenair (including Liverpool Flying School etc.)	02.03.1963	current
Cheshire Air Training School	12.06.1970	current
Ravenair	22.06.1998	current
VLM	23.02.2004	29.06.07
FlyBe	10.02.2005	03.09.07
WIZZair	07.12.2004	current
Flyglobespan	01.11.06	-
Air Malta	05.05.07	-

Appendix 5: Airline Types' First Visits to Liverpool

Date	Aircraft	Carrier and flight
16.06.30	G-AAEJArmstrong-Whitworth Argosy II	Imperial Airways, start of service
18.06.30	G-EBMR Handley Page W.10	Imperial Airways, scheduled service
25.06.30	G-EBIX Handley Page W.8F	Imperial Airways, scheduled service
01.07.31	G-EBTS Fokker F.VII	Private flight
18.03.32	G-AAXC Handley Page HP.42	Imperial Airways, charter flight
02.05.33	G-ACCE D.H.84 Dragon	Demonstration flight
14.08.33	G-ACGF Avro 618 Ten	Midland & Scottish Air Ferries, scheduled service
22.12.33	G-ACAE Ford 5-AT Trimotor	Landed for customs clearance
31.05.34	PH-AFV Fokker F.XII	KLM, for scheduled service next day
01.11.34	G-ACVY D.H.86 Express	RAS, scheduled service
01.12.34	G-ACPN D.H.89 Rapide	Hillman Airways, first scheduled service
25.05.35	PH-AKH Douglas DC-2	KLM, demonstration flight
25.01.37	G-ACRN Avro 652 (Anson)	Air pilot training flight
31.03.37	G-AEOI Lockheed 12A	Assembled after shipment from USA
11.07.38	PH-APE Lockheed 14	KLM, scheduled service
02.07.39	PH-ASR Douglas DC-3	KLM, scheduled service
04.07.40	G-AERU Junkers Ju 52/3m	Arrived for shipment to Africa by sea
02.08.41	DZ203 Boeing 247D	Delivery after shipment from USA
06.10.47	EI-AD-Vickers Viking	Aer Lingus, scheduled service

Date	Aircraft	Carrier and flight
20.03.48	EI-ADE Lockheed L.749 Constellation	Aer Linte, charter flight
20.03.48	G-AHJC Bristol 170 Freighter	Britavia, charter flight
02.06.49	NC90911 Douglas DC-4	Flying Tiger Line, GCA practice
20.05.50	PH-TEF Convair CV-240	KLM, diverted flight
10.07.51	G-ALZL D.H.114 Heron	BEA, demonstration flights
26.05.53	G-AMDB Dart-Dakota	Demonstration flights
	(first turbo-propeller aircraft)	
25.03.55	G-AMOC Vickers Viscount	Diverted flight
22.08.55	F-BELV Boeing 307 Stratoliner	UAT, charter flight
21.05.56	XB283 Blackburn Beverley C.1	Demonstration at air display
03.01.57	F-ZABT Nord Noratlas	Landed for customs clearance
20.01.58	G-ALHG Canadair C-4 Argonaut	BOAC, charter flight
23.04.58	LN-FOP Curtiss C-46R	Fred Olsen, charter flight
05.12.58	EI-AKB Fokker F-27 Friendship	Aer Lingus, demonstration flights
18.07.59	G-ALDI Handley Page Hermes 4	Britavia, charter flight
06.04.60	G-AMAH Airspeed Ambassador	Dan-Air, charter flight
08.06.60	F-BIAM Douglas DC-6B	UAT, charter flight
25.10.60	SP-LNB Ilyushin IL-14	LOT, charter flight
19.05.63	XN856 Armstrong-Whitworth	RAF
	AW660 Argosy C.1	
11.06.63	N304K Grumman Gulfstream I	Ford Motor Co.
18.07.63	G-APWA Handley Page Dart Herald Autair	Charter flight
01.01.64	G-AOVT Bristol Britannia 312	British Eagle, scheduled service
21.03.64	G-ARAY Hawker Siddeley HS.748	Private flight
28.06.64	G-ASCN Short Skyvan	Shorts
28.06.64	OY-KNC Douglas DC-7C	SAS, charter flight
04.09.64	G-APEK Vickers Vanguard	BEA, diverted flight
26.11.64	OO-SRC Sud SE.210 Caravelle	SABENA, charter flight
	(first pure-jet airliner)	
28.09.65	EI-ANH BAC 1-11	Aer Lingus, diverted flight
01.10.65	50019 Lockheed C-130 Hercules	USAF, training TA paratroops
05.07.66	EI-ANV Boeing 707-348	Aer Linte, charter flight
12.07.66	F-BHBI Lockheed L.1049	Air France, charter flight
	Super Constellation	
13.12.66	PH-LLE Lockheed Electra	KLM, charter flight
14.12.66	PH-DCF Douglas DC-8	KLM, charter flight
07.01.67	HB-IFA Douglas DC-9	Swissair, diverted flight
09.01.67	G-ARPS DH.121 Trident 1	BEA, diverted flight
10.01.67	G-ASGA Vickers Super VC-10	BOAC, diverted flight
17.02.67	G-APDO DH.106 Comet 4	Dan-Air, scheduled flight
26.04.67	XR364 Short Belfast C.1	Autoland development trials
21.10.67	G-AVRA Britten-Norman BN.2 Islander	Loganair, charter flight
15.07.68	HA-MOF Ilyushin IL-18	MALÉV, charter flight
17.02.69	G-ATXJ Handley Page Jetstream	Demonstration flight
24.05.69	EI-ASB Boeing 737	Aer Lingus, charter flight
27.05.69	N949K Beech 99A	Demonstration flight
01.07.69	CF-WTE DHC-6 Twin Otter	Demonstration flight

Date	Aircraft	Carrier and flight
23.08.69	G-AWGS Canadair CL-44	Freight charter flight
18.11.69	No.46 Nord 262	French Air Force, diverted flight
03.04.70	PH-MAT Fokker F-28 Fellowship	Martinair, charter flight
14.04.70	F-BKML Swearingen Merlin III	Private flight
19.10.70	YR-AMP Antonov An-24	TAROM, charter flight
20.11.72	G-AZZC Douglas DC-10 (first 'wide-body')	Laker, demonstration flights
11.12.72	DM-SCH Tupolev Tu-134	Interflug, charter flight
15.09.73	G-BAJW Boeing 727	Dan-Air, diverted flight
24.07.74	G-BAAB Lockheed L-1011 Tristar	Court Line, charter flight
27.01.76	G-BDMA Short SD.3-30	Manufacturer's trials
28.04.76	OO-TEG Airbus A-300B	Trans European Airways, charter flight
24.06.76	G-AZZM Britten-Norman Trislander	Loganair, technical stop for fuel
13.03.77	G-BFZK Embraer EMB-110 Bandeirante	Air Ecosse, technical stop for fuel
10.11.78	G-AWNI Boeing 747	British Airways, diverted flight
27.05.79	YR-TPB Tupolev Tu-154	TAROM, inclusive tour service
08.07.79	F-BPPA Aerospacelines Guppy 201	To collect A-300 wings, Set 101
26.08.79	F-BTSC Concorde	Air France, charter flight
29.05.80	EC-CTE Convair 990A	Spantax, diverted flight
28.06.80	00455 Lockheed C-5A Galaxy	USAF, demonstration flight
07.01.83	G-OBAE BAe 146	Route-proving flight
16.01.83	G-RMSS Short 360	Air Ecosse, positioned for schedule
26.09.83	G-MONC Boeing 757	Monarch, diverted flight
12.02.84	G-BKVZ Boeing 767	Britannia, crew training flight
01.02.85	G-BSFI SAAB 340A	Birmingham Executive, crew training
18.03.85	G-BRYB de Havilland DHC-7	Brymon Airways, charter flight
19.03.85	OE-LDU McDonnell Douglas MD-81	Austrian Airlines, charter flight
14.05.85	PH-AGB Airbus A-310	KLM, charter flight
28.01.86	LN-HPG Dornier Do 228	Norving, charter flight
13.08.87	PT-SIJ Embraer EMB-120 Brasilia	Demonstration flight
26.08.87	G-MATP BAe ATP	Manufacturer's trials
22.02.89	EI-FKA Fokker F-50	Aer Lingus, scheduled service
01.05.89	DDR-SEU Ilyushin IL-62M	Interflug, charter flight
06.11.89	EI-BXS ATR-42	Ryanair, scheduled flight
23.11.89	PH-ZCK Fokker F-100	Air Europe, crew training
06.05.90	YU-AOB Airbus A-320	Inclusive tour flight
11.10.90	LZ-INK Ilyushin IL-76	Freight charter
13.11.91	LZ-BAF Antonov An-12	Freight charter
30.11.91	G-BRYI de Havilland DHC-8	Brymon, charter flight
07.02.93	G-LOGJ BAe Jetstream 41	Loganair, crew training
20.06.93	YL-RAC Antonov An-26	Freight charter
14.12.93	RA-82042 Antonov An-124	Freight charter
12.08.94	G-VSKY Airbus A-340	Virgin Atlantic, crew training
02.02.95	OY-JRP Beech 1900	Charter flight
07.08.95	041 Yakolev Yak-40	Polish Air Force, charter flight
19.10.95	PH-MCR McDonnell-Douglas MD-11	Martinair, charter flight
13.12.95	EI-JFK Airbus A-330	Aer Lingus

Date	Aircraft	Carrier and flight
12.07.96	D-CATS Dornier Do 328	Diverted flight
04.10.96	HA-YFD L-410 Turbolet	Charter flight
27.12.96	HB-IZW SAAB 2000	Crossair, diverted flight
25.07.97	G-EMBA Embraer EMB-145	Crew training
03.08.97	D-ACLL Canadair RJ (Regional Jet)	Diverted flight
26.04.00	9A-CTH Airbus A-319	Charter flight
30.10.00	UR-BYH Antonov An-72	Emerald flight on charter
20.10.02	G-YMMM Boeing 777-236ER	Charter flight
10.08.03	D-ABOF Dornier Do 328JET	Charter flight
19.07.05	SU-EAJ Tupolev Tu 204	TNT Freight flight
01.08.05	YL-LBT Yakolev Yak-42	Passenger charter (football team)

Appendix 6: Concorde at Liverpool

Liverpool received twenty-two visits by Concorde, far more than the majority of UK regional airports. A major reason for this has been the annual Grand National Race meeting, usually held in April, which has attracted a number of charter flights, initially from Paris by Air France but later including regular subsonic visits by British Airways Concordes from London. While at Liverpool the opportunity has been taken by fifteen of the BA aircraft to operate supersonic flights over to the North Sea for the local air-minded population and for people from further afield in the north west of England and north Wales. The actual Concorde operations are as follows:

Date	Airline	Registration	From/To	Notes
26.08.79	AF	F-BTSC	Paris Charles de Gaulle	
30.03.80	AF	F-BVFB	Paris Charles de Gaulle	
24.09.83	BA	G-BOAF	London Heathrow	
06.04.85	AF	F-BVFA	Paris Charles de Gaulle	
05.04.86	BA	G-BOAD	London Heathrow	Two local flights
03.10.86	BA	G-BOAD	New York JFK-Heathrow	
06/07.12.86	BA	G-BOAB	Birmingham-Heathrow	One local, night stopped
04.04.87	BA	G-BOAE	London Heathrow	Two local flights
04.04.87	BA	G-BOAA	London Heathrow	Two local flights
09.04.88	BA	G-BOAE	London Heathrow	Four local flights
09/10.04.88	BA	G-BOAD	London Heathrow	Two local, night stopped
08.04.89	BA	G-BOAE	London Heathrow	
06.04.91	BA	G-BOAG	London Heathrow	One local
06.06.92	BA	G-BOAD	London Heathrow	One local
03.04.93	BA	G-BOAG	London Heathrow	One local
09.04.94	BA	G-BOAC	London Heathrow	One local
08.04.95	BA	G-BOAD	London Heathrow	One local
30.03.96	BA	G-BOAG	London Heathrow	One local
05.04.97	BA	G-BOAB	London Heathrow	One local
30.08.97	AF	F-BTSD	Paris CDG-Manchester	
04.04.98	BA	G-BOAG	London Heathrow	One local
10.04.99	BA	G-BOAA	London Heathrow	One local

The first Concorde flight was by the aircraft that was tragically lost after take-off from Paris in July 2000. In 1979, the flight was the first Air France charter to the UK and the first charter flight by a Concorde outside London, all previous flights from or to other points having been diversions to Prestwick or Manchester. 1983 saw the first visit of a British Airways Concorde in the airport's fiftieth anniversary year. This flight was the first BA Concorde charter to a provincial airport and the first to a non-BA station.

In October 1986, the arrival of the transatlantic flight from New York, with returning passengers from a QE2 cruise, was the first Concorde to use the then-new terminal building. 1987 saw two Concordes on the tarmac at the same time and this was followed the next year by two more operating between them four subsonic and six supersonic flights over the weekend carrying in all nearly 1,000 passengers. Altogether a total of eighty-eight Concorde movements have taken place at Liverpool. The 'local' flights (flights departing from and returning to the original departure point) were supersonic experience flights for charter passengers, usually made over the North Sea.

Appendix 7: Traffic Figures Table

Year	Total Passengers	Total Freight (tons)	Total Mail (tons)	Air Transport Movements (Airline landings & take-offs)
		Blank entries indicate that information is not available.		
1933	3,642			
1934	5,145			
1935	17,114			
1936	16,038	10,729		
1937	13,508	8,927		
1938	12,577			
1939	8,470	41	157	5,456
1940	14,189	24	97	2,941
1941				
1942	19,075	25	144	3,395
1943				
1944				
1945	50,944			
1946	59,173			
1947	66,058			
1948	74,795	7,893		
1949	83,352	6,862		
1950	77,204			
1951	83,352			
1952	83,755			
1953	87,683			
1954	102,544			
1955	123,776	944		
1956	141,552	617		
1957	150,100	563		
1958	136,681	640		
1959	135,701	675		

Year	Total Passengers	Total Freight (tons)	Total Mail (tons)	Air Transport Movements (Airline landings & take-offs)
1960	177,177	3,606	734	8,291
1961	251,415	5,397	784	11,431
1962	293,293	4,115	718	12,899
1963	311,007	7,977	735	13,258
1964	375,495	8,849	768	14,562
1965	444,682	9,475	813	16,932
1966	479,844	16,639	1,108	19,757
1967	477,125	14,521	884	17,767
1968	454,088	16,501	745	18,414
1969	411,228	17,502	722	16,767
1970	441,341	19,912	478	15,303
1971	519,233	15,750	366	14,805
1972	544,106	17,139	360	15,764
1973	586,723	18,056	391	16,078
1974	519,233	16,912	398	14,950
1975	450,101	13,598	345	12,255
1976	359,560	15,671	323	11,286
1977	276,603	11,935	239	8,720
1978	303,066	9,312	232	10,113
1979	617,947	20,367	2,157	16,687
1980	387,250	13,727	7,743	16,937
1981	283,396	9,285	9,327	16,658
1982	254,151	9,995	12,485	21,599
1983	239,708	9,398	11,541	20,857
1984	231,813	9,277	11,139	18,700
1985	260,214	9,233	12,189	17,901
1986	264,975	6,981	13,155	19,628
1987	341,591	1,405	12,181	18,421
1988	360,078	3,030	11,874	18,249
1989	488,266	23,842 combined		21,151
1990	516,373	13,187	13,060	23,805
1991	488,208	13,292	12,674	21,711
1992	466,534	10,226	12,738	18,457
1993	470,399	15,184	13,703	18,900
1994	444,534	25,364	15,089	20,833
1995	506,723	31,594	14,435	23,421
1996	626,101	28,440	16,538	27,039
1997	691,157	26,186	17,244	28,575
1998	875,222	25,457	16,351	28,649
1999	1,307,515	25,389	16,788	27,093
2000	1,986,589	29,657	17,134	32,475
2001	2,258,341	23,141	16,572	32,403
2002	2,839,636	14,883	17,016	
2003	3,180,801	12,543	15,760	
2004	3,335,839	9,467	7,569	
2005	4,416,751	8,649	6,373	
2006	4,971,452	5,792	4,243	

Additional Information Sources

Readers who wish to keep up to date with events at Liverpool John Lennon Airport may wish to know of the following sources:

Friends of Liverpool Airport (FoLA)

FoLA was formed in 1980 at a time when the very existence of the airport remained in doubt. It was a time when few saw a need for it, with Manchester 'just down the road', and fewer still wanting to invest in it. Its four clear objectives, set early on, are:

1   To promote the use of, and the need for, Liverpool Airport.
2   To encourage the preservation, development and improvement of the airport and its facilities.
3   To educate public opinion and give advice and information about the airport and the services from it.
4   To promote civic pride in Liverpool Airport.

As the society grew it beavered away, largely in the background, doing whatever was required to help and support the airport. In the early days, members could be found helping with the catering, organising events such as open days and air shows, printing timetables, and even cutting the grass. As the airport developed through the 1980s and 1990s so did the role of FoLA with the emphasis moving to publicity and promotion. One of the major projects FoLA undertook in the 1990s was helping the airport mount a rebuttal of the need for a second runway at Manchester at the subsequent planning inquiry. Although the airport is today a fully staffed, heavily invested facility with its own expertise, FoLA still plays a part with its members being called upon to help with 'one-off' events such as wheelchair-pushing when flights to Lourdes operate. A recent development has been the introduction of Airport Tours, which are now being led by security-cleared FoLA members. FoLA is always on the look out for new members. Membership starts from just £12 per year with a substantial quarterly newsletter sent out by post. FoLA holds monthly meetings at the airport, usually with a guest speaker, and has a website at www.fola.org.uk. Application for membership can be made from the website or by writing to FoLA, c/o Liverpool John Lennon Airport, Liverpool L24 1YD.

The Jetstream Club

The Jetstream Club is based at the Marriott South Hotel, the former Speke Airport Terminal Building. It was formed in 2002 to save, preserve and then display the fourth Jetstream 41 prototype, G-JMAC. The club is based at the site of the original Liverpool 'Speke' Airport, now a fabulous Marriott Hotel. A flight simulator was installed in 2004 with over 100 different aircraft that can be 'flown' from the flight-deck. The club also has a Grumman/Yankee AA1 aircraft with a unique registration, G-SEXY. Quite a few ladies like to have their photograph taken standing next to it! The Jetstream Club is also home to Bristol Britannia, G-ANCF, 'Charlie Fox'. First flown in 1958, the aircraft is owned by the Britannia Aircraft Preservation Trust. Charlie Fox is currently undergoing an extensive restoration, which will see the aircraft back in the British Eagle colours that it wore when flying from Liverpool and is expected to be fully on display by the end of 2008. The restoration is being handled by the Jetstream Club's dedicated volunteers. See: www.jetstream-club. org. (Registered Charity No.1106923)

Liverpool Airport website

The official LJLA website provided by Liverpool Airport PLC giving details of services, access routes, car parking information, and everything else that intending passengers need to know. Go to: www.liverpoolairport.com.

North West Air News

Website and forum (webmaster Dave Graham). This website provides comprehensive details of LJLA activities, with a monthly review of news and operations by all the airlines that fly to and from the airport, traffic statistics, details of resident aircraft, interesting visitors, and photographs of events going back over many years. The discussion forum provides details of day-to-day events in and around LJLA. See: http://www.nwan.co.uk.

Rapide

The magazine for the north-west aero enthusiast, which publishes articles on aviation history in the north-west, and is available from Coulton-Lewis Communications (e-mail: starflite@dsl.pipex. com) c/o 7 Lawn Drive, Upton, Chester CH2 1ER. The magazine is produced on a non-profit making basis, between two and four times a year.